TWAYNE'S WORLD AUTHORS SERIES

A Survey of the World's Literature

Sylvia E. Bowman, Indiana University

GENERAL EDITOR

SWITZERLAND

Ulrich Weisstein, Indiana University

EDITOR

Friedrich Dürrenmatt

(TWAS 87)

TWAYNE'S WORLD AUTHORS SERIES (TWAS)

*The purpose of TWAS is to survey the major writers
—novelists, dramatists, historians, poets, philosophers,
and critics—of the nations of the world. Among the
national literatures covered are those of Australia,
Canada, China, Eastern Europe, France, Germany,
Greece, India, Italy, Japan, Latin America, New Zea-
land, Poland, Russia, Scandinavia, Spain, Switzerland
and the African nations, as well as Hebrew, Yiddish,
and Latin Classical literatures. This survey is com-
plemented by Twayne's United States Authors Series
and English Authors Series.*

*The intent of each volume in these series is to present
a critical-analytical study of the works of the writer;
to include biographical and historical material that
may be necessary for understanding, appreciation,
and critical appraisal of the writer; and to present all
material in clear, concise English—but not to vitiate
the scholarly content of the work by doing so.*

Friedrich Dürrenmatt

By MURRAY B. PEPPARD
Amherst College

Twayne Publishers, Inc.   ::   New York

Library of Congress Catalog Card Number: 70–79212

To Jo

FRIEDRICH DÜRRENMATT

Preface

OF living dramatists writing in German, the Swiss playwright Friedrich Dürrenmatt was the most frequently staged in Germany during the theater season of 1965–66. In 1965 his *The Physicists* was among the most frequently staged and most favorably received plays of the season. Even in 1963, the year of the Gerhart Hauptmann centenary, Dürrenmatt was third in the total number of productions. In America, three of his plays have been chosen for inclusion in the annual publication *The Best Plays*.[1] Many of Dürrenmatt's plays, stories, and radio plays have been translated into English, produced on Broadway, and broadcast on television. The number and popularity of the school texts of his plays edited for the use of students learning German has made him a "modern classic" in our classrooms. Translations into languages other than English have assured him an international reputation unique among contemporary representatives of German culture.

Dürrenmatt's success and continuing popularity date from the early 1950's. In barely two years he had three *premières* at the Munich Kammerspiele: *The Marriage of Mr. Mississippi* in March, 1952; *Nocturnal Conversation with a Despised Person* in July, 1952; and *An Angel Comes to Babylon* in December, 1953. There had been earlier productions in Germany; but it was this series and its acceptance by the public that constituted the real breakthrough to success. These performances also provide the background for the lecture tour on which Dürrenmatt read his *Problems of the Theater*. His first Swiss success was *Romulus the Great;* the first success in West Germany, *The Marriage of Mr. Mississippi;* but the first international success did not come until the season of 1957–58 when *The Visit* was triumphantly staged in London and New York. Prizes and honors have come to Dürrenmatt in such profusion that they have become a source of embarrassment. In 1956 he received the Prize of the War Blind for his radio play *Traps;* in 1958 the Prix d'Italia for the radio play *An Evening in Late Fall;* and in the same year the literature prize of the *Tribune de Lausanne* for *Traps;* in 1959 the Critics' Prize of New York and the Schiller Prize of the city of Mannheim, as well as a citation from the city of Bern for "The Pledge," and in 1960 the prize of the Swiss Schiller Foundation, the highest accolade of all. It is unnecessary to list all the lesser honors which have been bestowed on Dürrenmatt; it would also be one-sided to do so, since he has had his full share of carping criticism, unnecessary and unprovoked sensationalism in newspapers and periodicals, and other flurries of adverse publicity. As neither the praise nor the blame has been directly solicited, Dürrenmatt himself has kept calm and unruffled through it all, and has responded by preserving his sense of humor, both with regard to himself and to his works. He has conducted himself with wit and dignity, and most important of all, he has consistently refused to interpret himself or to identify himself with an ideology..

The works themselves, however, are not reserved and quiet; they are deliberately provocative and challenging, and have been a constant source of controversy. Dürrenmatt has sought to shock his contemporaries out of their smugness and stir their consciences. In presenting plays that deal with contemporary problems, he has not hesitated to use drastic means such as grotesque exaggeration, parody, slapstick satire, and cabaret tricks. He is rightly called "uncomfortable" by the critics,[2] a satisfying epithet for a playwright who wishes to arouse and excite and who has nothing but scorn for literature that soothes and comforts. Modern man is on trial in Dürrenmatt's works; all his heroes—usually passive, "negative" heroes who endure rather than conquer—are tried, tested, and forced to make moral decisions in a confused world which they do not understand but must withstand.

Dürrenmatt has always been reticent about his own person. In interviews he has consistently maintained that a writer's essential biography consists of his works. We shall accept this point of view in this book, respect the privacy he desires, and deal with his works rather than with the details of his life. A biography in the usual sense of the term will thus not be presented, but rather the growth and development of one of the great modern dramatists. The already extensive critical literature on Dürrenmatt has been used throughout the book, but references to the clamor of conflicting voices referred to above will be made only where it seems pertinent. His fame is beyond question; and our attention will be focused on his works.

The book is organized as follows. The first chapter deals briefly with Dürrenmatt's early prose, concentrating on the characteristics already evident even in his first, imitative stage. The second chapter discusses his early plays, while the third chapter presents a more detailed study of his masterpieces, the plays on which his reputation rests. The fourth chapter offers a discussion of his radio plays, the fifth treats Dürrenmatt's short stories, and the sixth and last discusses his critical writings, concluding with an attempt to evaluate his stature as a dramatist and his place in contemporary literature.

Acknowledgments

Special thanks are due to Jo Peppard for her patient proofreading and suggestions for stylistic improvements. It is a great pleasure to acknowledge the tireless and tolerant help of Roxanne McCabe, who typed the manuscript.

Contents

FRIEDRICH DÜRRENMATT

by

MURRAY B. PEPPARD

The Swiss dramatist Friedrich Dürrenmatt has acquired international fame as
a playwright of great stature. His plays
have been translated into many languages
and performed with acclaim throughout
the world. Several of his plays have been
successfully presented on Broadway, and
some have become part of the standard
repetoire of college theaters in this country. His essays have been influential in
drama studies both here and abroad. His
detective stories and radio plays have attained considerable popularity in German-speaking countries and several of
them have been adapted for television.
The number and popularity of the school
texts edited for the use of students learning German has made him a modern classic in our classrooms, so that a knowledge
of his works is becoming increasingly important for students of German literature
as well as for lovers of the theater.

This is the first full-length treatment of
the writer Dürrenmatt, both as creative
author and critic, which has appeared in
English. Since Dürrenmatt has always
firmly insisted that he has no biography,
the stages of his development and his
growing stature as author form the main
concern of this book. From his early short
stories to his latest plays the important
themes and motifs are carefully examined

Chronology

1921   January 5, Friedrich Dürrenmatt born in Konolfingen (Canton Bern), Switzerland. His father, Reinhold Dürrenmatt, was a Protestant minister. His grandfather, Ulrich Dürrenmatt, had been active in politics and was also known as a popular satirist.

1933–   Attended secondary school in the neighboring town of
1935   Grosshochstetten.

1935   The family moved to Bern, where Dürrenmatt attended the *Gymnasium.*

1941   Beginning of study at the university, first at Zurich, then in Bern. Literature and philosophy were his main fields; he also painted a great deal, and read widely, becoming acquainted with the works of Aristophanes, the Greek tragedians, Kierkegaard, Heym, Trakl, Kafka, and Ernst Jünger.

1943   His first literary experiments in drama and narrative prose. Continuation of his studies, especially philosophy, and of his amateur painting and drawing.

1945   His first short story, "The Old Man," published in a newspaper in Bern. Composition of the stories "The Picture of Sisyphos," "The Manager of the Theater," and start of the play *It Is Written.*

1946   The play *It Is Written* completed. The stories "The Trap" and "Pilate" and the first radio play, *The Double,* finished.

1947   Married Lotti Geissler. In April is *première* of *It Is Written* at Schauspielhaus, Zurich. In the same year, the play is published as a book with illustrations by Dürrenmatt. Beginning of work on *The Blind Man* and on a "novel," now published as a fragmentary story, "The City."

1948   January 10, the *première* of *The Blind Man* in Basel. Start of work on the play *Romulus the Great.* Dürrenmatt moved to Ligerz, began work on a play tentatively entitled *The*

Tower of Babel, which remained unfinished and was later destroyed. In October a Dürrenmatt play produced in Germany for the first time: *Romulus the Great* is presented in Göttingen.

1950 Work on the detective story "The Judge and His Executioner," which appeared serially in the periodical *Der Schweizerische Beobachter*. Started composing the play *The Marriage of Mr. Mississippi*.

1951 The second detective story, "The Suspicion," published serially. Wrote the radio play *The Case of the Donkey's Shadow* and the prose sketch "The Dog." Start of his activity as theater critic for *Die Weltwoche* of Zurich (continued until 1952).

1952 Moved to a home in Neuchâtel. In March the *première* of *The Marriage of Mr. Mississippi* in the Kammerspiele in Munich. Completion of the story "The Tunnel" and publication of his early prose in book form: *The City*. Wrote the radio plays *Stranitzky and the National Hero* and *Nocturnal Conversation with a Despised Person*. First foreign presentation of a Dürrenmatt play: *Les Fous de Dieu* (*It Is Written*) in Paris.

1953 Completion of *An Angel Comes to Babylon; première* in Munich in December.

1954 Completion of the radio plays *Hercules and the Augean Stables* and *Operation Vega*.

1955 *Problems of the Theater*, originally the text for a series of lectures presented in Switzerland and West Germany during late 1954 and early 1955, published in book form. Finished the story "Once a Greek" and the play *The Visit*.

1956 *Première* of *The Visit* in Zurich. Wrote the radio play *Traps* (later a story, then adapted for television), the radio play *An Evening in Late Fall*, and recast *The Marriage of Mr. Mississippi*. In October Dürrenmatt staged *The Visit* in Basel.

1957 Rewrote for television the story "The Judge and His Executioner" and composed the film text "It Happened in Broad Daylight," which was later reworked as the story "The Pledge." New versions of the plays *An Angel Comes to Babylon* and *Romulus the Great* for the first edition of *Comedies I. The Visit* performed in England.

Chronology

1958   Start of work on *Frank V* together with the Swiss composer Paul Burkhard. During the winter *Mississippi* performed off Broadway under the title *Fools Are Passing Through*. In May production of *The Visit* in New York.

1959   In March the *première* of *Frank V* in Zurich. In November Dürrenmatt received the Schiller Prize of the city of Mannheim.

1960   *The Visit* continues to be staged outside of Switzerland. A film version of *The Marriage of Mr. Mississippi* produced in Germany. *The Deadly Game*, a play by James Yaffe based on "Traps" produced on Broadway. *Frank V* recast for the Munich production.

1961   Completion of *The Physicists*. Publication of first edition of collected radio plays. A third version of *Romulus the Great* published in *Spectaculum IV*.

1962   In February the *première* of *The Physicists* in Zurich; Berlin, Munich, Hamburg and Hanover follow during the same season. The radio play *Hercules and the Augean Stables* rewritten as a stage play. Gore Vidal's adaptation of *Romulus the Great* produced on Broadway.

1963   *The Physicists* produced in London in January; performances in other countries follow during the year. In March the *première* of *Hercules and the Augean Stables* in Zurich. *Comedies II* published.

1964   A new version of *Frank V* prepared for production by Dürrenmatt in Bochum, but not performed. A revised version of *Romulus the Great* prepared for the stage. *The Physicists* in New York in Kirkup's translation, October and November; also staged in Cleveland and Baltimore during the season of 1964–65. Start of work on *The Meteor*.

1965   Revised version of *Romulus the Great* performed in Stuttgart.

1966   In January the *première* of *The Meteor* in Zurich; several German cities produce the play during the season. Elisabeth Brock-Sulzer collects and edits *Essays and Speeches on the Theater*.

1967   In March the revised version of *It Is Written*, entitled *The Anabaptists*, staged in Zurich. In May *The Meteor* performed for the Berlin Theater Meeting 1967.

both for their intrinsic merit and for their relationship to contemporary German-language drama. The already extensive critical literature has been consulted and is frequently cited in order to give a balanced picture of his place in contemporary letters.

CHAPTER 1

The Years of Apprenticeship: The Early Prose

Culture is no excuse.

IT was not until 1952, a year of success and acclaim for his stage productions, that Dürrenmatt collected his early prose works and published them in one volume with the title *The City*. By this time, his reputation as a dramatist was being established not only in his native Switzerland, but in Germany as well. Most of the stories and sketches which make up the volume were composed between 1943 and 1946, but were repeatedly reworked until 1952. Thus even this collection illustrates Dürrenmatt's well-known urge to rewrite, revise, and correct. In the afterword, Dürrenmatt states that the collection is not to be evaluated as an attempt to create narrative prose, but rather as a necessary form of self-discipline and orientation. They represent, he claims, a kind of struggle with himself; and he adds, with a turn of phrase anticipating a characteristic of his later writings, that it was a struggle which could only have meaning if it were unsuccessful. In a philosophical sense, the stories represent Dürrenmatt's attempts to overcome a kind of modish nihilism and a tendency to indulge in the bizarre and macabre for its own sake. The book is clearly written in an immature style, but for the student of Dürrenmatt it is important for two reasons: first, for the influences that are evident and not yet completely assimilated; and second, for the basic viewpoints which emerge in these early works and continue, often in more fully developed and sophisticated form, throughout all of his artistic career.

The first influence perceptible in all the stories, except perhaps the last ("The Tunnel"), is that of Kafka. It is a Kafkaesque world into which the reader enters. There is the same sense of indirect confession, the same narrow focus on a schematized reality that is at the same time bewildering in its ramifications and totally in-

17

scrutable; and there is the same seemingly senseless search on the part of the protagonist, the feeling of being lost and totally estranged in an environment that becomes more hostile with every descriptive detail. A sense of futility and frustration emerges from these imitative stories as it does from Kafka's works. Dürrenmatt actually seems to model his style on Kafka's aphorisms.

If the view of the world is the narrowly selective and slightly distorted view familiar from Kafka, the style is, sentence by sentence, reminiscent not of Kafka's periods but of the expository prose of Ernst Jünger. The short, declarative sentences, which are monotonous when sustained, contain striking, yet also palpably forced imagery. Dürrenmatt apparently learned from the terse and didactic style of Jünger's *The Adventurous Heart*. The use of this basic prose style, originally fashioned to transmit observations in the form of essays, and replete with condensed, aphoristic formulations, in combination with an urge to evoke scenery and events which are surrealistically weird and macabre, leads to stylistic infelicities on almost every page. To cite just one example: "The stars are yellow. The moon is brown." [1]

Although in these works form and content are in open and obvious conflict, there are indications that Dürrenmatt was gradually finding the language adequate to his needs. There are themes and human responses that are peculiarly his own. In the first sketch, "Christmas," there is a human gesture unlike any to be found in Kafka or Jünger, for there is a moment of sympathy and participation in the life of another human being. In the last story there is an emotional achievement quite foreign to his models, namely a moment of supreme serenity of soul; and Dürrenmatt has suddenly found the uniquely apposite language in which to describe it. Thus Dürrenmatt's characteristics are evident in this collection, even where they are overlaid with foreign elements— from which he freed himself in a remarkably short time; and they are all the more easily identified for the strange costume in which they appear. Certain traits which we associate with Dürrenmatt, however, are still not completely developed. As befits an author engaged in a struggle with nihilism, the humor in these stories is usually grim and cold, whereas the mature works witness a freer, more liberating laughter. Dürrenmatt had not yet learned to use the grotesque significantly, nor had he learned to have his pathos and at the same time undercut it with irony. Many of the stories are told in the first person, but the narrator seems remote and impersonal, and more like a "K." of Kafka than a living voice that invites or establishes intimacy in a dialogue with the reader. Even the attempts to breathe animation and life into the stories are often forced and awkward, as may be seen in some of the inept personifications such as "The houses creep across the ground." [2]

In spite of the author's attempts to create an environment that can be visualized with a strange mixture of techniques, and despite a wealth of observed details, the stories remain abstract. They are merely frameworks of conceptualizations. The sustained exaggeration and the accumulation of rich, lush adjectives only serve to underline the skeletal quality of the sketches. There are epic possibilities in stories like "The Director of the Theater," with its faint echoes of Jünger's *On the Marble Cliffs*, but the narrative element is not fully developed, remains on the level of a sketch or outline, and is overburdened with efforts at producing an atmosphere. The story "The Torturer" is interesting because it portrays the person inflicting the torture, not the victim, and is thus remotely reminiscent of Kafka's "In the Penal Colony." Unfortunately, the prose remains on the level of assertion and does not achieve real contours of depiction. Dreadful things are asserted and hinted at, but not concretely enough portrayed to be visualized. The reader is so conscious of the effect on the narrator that his own perception of what is allegedly happening is diminished and suffers from being filtered through the reactions of the narrator. Since the sting of the events is removed by their passage through the medium of an interposed narrator, the reader is frequently left with fuzzy and vague impressions. It is strange that a dramatist, with his eye for scenic configurations, should convey, in this early prose, only the effect on the depicted observer, not on the people in action.

The abstract nature of these stories may be ascribed, in part, to the fact that many of them, such as "The Torturer" and "The Dog," are expressly stated to be allegories. The visual inspiration for some of the allegory, and its intended suggestiveness, are derived from the grotesque paintings of Hieronymus Bosch. Dürrenmatt's interest in painting is well-known; at this period of his development he still seems to have been a painter at heart. But he has not yet learned to paint with words. Dürrenmatt, soon to become a master of the grotesque in his plays, is in these early prose sketches so deeply involved in the attempt to create a macabre effect that the contrastive element so basic to the significantly grotesque is completely lacking. Pure, unrelieved horror, as for example in the story "The Trap," with its suggestions of apocalyptic self-torture, achieves only the effect of cruelty and the sensation of terror, not the balanced and mixed effect of the grotesque. What is missing is the bold humor and pervasive irony of the later plays. The wit and brilliance of repartee, which we associate with the dramatist Dürrenmatt, is entirely lacking, except in the final story, "The Tunnel."

"The Tunnel" was written in 1952, much later than the other stories (but not later than their revisions), and is humorous and ironic in a manner familiar from the plays. The story is not told in the first person; and perhaps for this very reason it is a cryptic self-portrait. The central character is a gentle and humorous caricature of Dürrenmatt himself. By a series of trivial traits, slowly built up to full portrait size, the personality of the traveler on his strange trip into the center of the earth takes on firm contours. The fantastic and fateful experience is presented, this time, in such a way that the reader can share both in the horror and the exhilaration of the adventure. The humorous details are developed cumulatively, as for example in the continued and seemingly normal functioning of the bureaucracy and the maintenance of an apparently normal routine, in spite of the most extraordinary technical mishap. This contrastive technique is a precursor of the style of Dürrenmatt's plays. For the first time, the hand of the master is visible.

Even more significant for the future than the stylistic mastery of contrastive techniques are the themes of "The Tunnel." The serenity and inner calm which result from the characters' acceptance of the catastrophe and their confident yielding to fate are important and will recur in later plays. Divine grace may be achieved by an individual who ceases his struggle to master the world and surrenders to his destiny. The almost euphoric buoyancy which the hero feels as he falls is at one and the same time a striking contrast to the expected physical response and a token of inner religious faith in a divine ordering of the world. The theme of disaster due to technical failure is linked here with the failure of the bureaucrats, who do not even recognize the failure, much less the miracle. Dürrenmatt's symbolism is unobtrusive and suggestive in a man-

ner which he was able to repeat only in his best writing. The fall
down the tunnel is felt as a falling into God's hands, thereby sug-
gesting—an overt statement would have destroyed the effect—
that the center of the earth is God's domain.

Since the word "grotesque" is an important word in any discussion of Dürrenmatt, who has become the foremost practitioner
and theorist of the grotesque drama in the German language today, it is appropriate to define this key term and distinguish it
from such related terms as "comic" or "absurd." Wolfgang Kayser,
whose indispensable study *The Grotesque in Painting and Poetry*[3]
has established the use of the word in its present sense, states that
the essential nature of the grotesque is the viewpoint which sees
the insecurity of man in a world only superficially ordered and
understood, a world in which the irrational and demonic may, at
any moment, break through the veneer of convention and compla-
cency to reveal fundamental and frightening truths. The grotesque has a mixed effect, turning laughter into horror, provoking
a smile and then suddenly causing it to freeze on the face of the
spectator. In its significant use it serves to unmask our everyday
world and what passes as normal reality in order to confront us
with the higher truths that have lain hidden. It is an attempt to
exorcise the demonic by means of the apparently comic or ridiculous, producing a shock effect as the deeper, irrational truth
emerges from behind a comic mask. Margret Dietrich, in a discussion of the grotesque in modern drama, considers a tragic view of
the world as the presupposition for the grotesque in art. The grotesque appears "like an explosion of unbearable tensions, a painful
and extreme manifestation of the helplessness of man, out of
which tragic laughter arises." [4]

In the commentary appended to the play *Frank V*, Dürrenmatt
specifically rejects the absurd theater, asserting that his plots are
not to be considered as absurd, since absurdity in the theater has
no serious content. The terms "absurd" and "grotesque" are unfortunately often confused with one another.[5] The absurd theater,
according to Wolfgang Hildesheimer,[6] one of its leading German
exponents, is based on resignation with regard to the effectiveness
of the theater and implies a renunciation of any attempt to teach
or demonstrate anything but man's folly and sense of being lost in
a ridiculous world. The absurd theater tends to be abstract and
symbolic. The bare mechanics of life are presented in situations

that are symbolic caricatures of reality. In the grotesque drama, on the contrary, the starting point is a model or stage representation of reality in recognizable, non-allegorical form, and it is only after the semblance of normal reality has been established in concrete form that, by means of contrastive technique, disorientation and estrangement from reality may be accomplished.

It is not only the beginning of Dürrenmatt's grasp of the technique of the grotesque which makes these stories interesting, for themes that will be important in the later plays are present in profusion. They have not yet received their final artistic formulation, but they point toward later developments. The statement in "The Director of the Theater" that guilt and atonement are only possible in a state of freedom anticipates more significant applications of a principle merely stated here and not transformed into artistic expression. "The Trap" represents in bald, crudely fashioned form an attitude toward life which, in a more sophisticated presentation, underlies many of the author's later works. The urge for self-torture, and the search for meaning in life through torment, crime, and suffering, reflect the world view of Dürrenmatt in its undeveloped and unadorned—one might almost say in its preliterary—form. The thought that daily life, if seen from a religious perspective, is a scene of moral torment and contains the seeds of suffering and atonement, is fruitful for the later, more polished works. The roots of what is grotesque in Dürrenmatt lie in a sensitive conscience and an acute awareness of man's fate and moral condition. An awareness of death and its ultimate moral meaning is apparent even in this early prose and has already found its final and constant symbol in the figure of the executioner.

There are many scenes in these stories which point toward later utilization in more finished artistic form. A section on pages 66 and 67 of "The Director of the Theater" anticipates *The Visit;* sections of *The City* which portray the city as a faceless and impersonal creature full of fear and threats anticipate not only *The Visit* and its portrayal of a community, but also shorter pieces such as the prose tale "Once a Greek." As it stands, *The City* represents an attempt to achieve effects like those of Kafka's prose, with visual elements borrowed from George Grosz and Hieronymus Bosch; but at the same time it anticipates later and more subtle portrayals of community relations. The successful communication of *hor-*

ror vitae and the sense of loathing, suffering, and self-inflicted pain prepare the way for an understanding of the later works, in which the horror is partially resolved in humor, and the grim and gruesome aspects are relieved by wit, so that the characteristically grotesque appears. From a study of these early works one can see that the scurrilous inspirations ("Einfälle") that form the plot basis for Dürrenmatt's stories are combined with a very serious purpose, namely the revelation of man's potential for sin and atonement. "We must be tortured in order for us to obtain insight, and an answer will come only to our cry of pain." [7] It is a sure sign of this early prose that the quotation is not effectively woven into the fabric of the narrative, but remains isolated as an aphoristic insight. Dürrenmatt soon learned to build his plots on such insights; but apparently he had to pass through his own dialectics of despair before he could free himself sufficiently to achieve the grotesque humor and the comic effects of his mature works.

What was needed in order to achieve this liberation from the style of his early prose was not irony and distance—Dürrenmatt already possessed them in abundance—but a method of communicating his message indirectly and by suggestion. Wellwarth says of the later Dürrenmatt: "Dürrenmatt may be characterized as a man with something to say who does not wish to be caught saying it." [8] Dürrenmatt has always emphatically rejected any notion that he is purveying a philosophy or message and has constantly asserted the primacy of *theater* in his plays. Religion and art are incommensurable fields of thought and action for Dürrenmatt; and art is not an adequate form of expression for religious faith. Only by indirect means, by suggestion and the implied sense of the action can religious attitudes be expressed in a work of art. [9] One can trace the development of this belief in the different functions of art and religion in the collected prose of *The City;* but in "The Tunnel" the message is given in the form which has remained characteristic for Dürrenmatt throughout his career. There are religious implications in the story, most insistently at the end, where the autobiographical hero achieves a euphoric sense of security and serenity in yielding to his fate. This feeling of confidence—or salvation—stems from an implicit faith that he is literally falling into God's hand; but the moral, or message, is not explicitly stated, since it is only made evident by the responses and actions of the person concerned.

Dürrenmatt's early prose can now be seen as a dead end. The technique of communicating his ideas through the visualized actions of people marks the next stage of his development. What is established in these sketches is the basic world view of the dramatist and his concern with central themes and motifs which will be the enduring substance of the later dramas and stories. Lonely and isolated man confronts the enigma of the universe and its monstrous complexity; and his ridiculously inadequate attempts to understand it—or even a small, private part of it—lead to ludicrous defeat. Efforts to guide or control even a small segment of the world are doomed to failure. But man's inadequacy and the inscrutability of the world do not lead to a pessimistic view of the world. This is the central paradox in Dürrenmatt's writing, for in spite of all appearances to the contrary, pessimism and resignation are not the proper responses to man's condition. The futility and frustration which result from man's striving might seem to relate Dürrenmatt's outlook to Kafka's, whose prose has exerted such a strong influence on him. But Dürrenmatt has a deeply religious faith in God, even if His ways with man are inscrutable and beyond human understanding. And he also has an awareness of death that is different from Kafka's. These two philosophical views, together with Dürrenmatt's sense of a divine ordering of the universe maintained in the face of repeated failures to participate in this order, distinguish one author from the other. They share the same sense of being excluded from the world order as long as man strives for a goal and tries to interfere with it; but they are poles apart in the emotional response to this situation; for instead of despair, frustration, and futility that find no resolution, Dürrenmatt progresses to hilarious fun, mockery, and laughter— laughter on the verge of an eschatological abyss—in a word, to a grotesque grasp of reality. It is not only disillusioned detachment and ironic distance which enable him to achieve this humorous view of the world, but also a profound faith in the possibility of divine grace.[10]

CHAPTER 2

The Early Plays

I am a Protestant and protest.

AT the *première* of *It Is Written* in Zurich in April, 1947, there were demonstrations and disturbances in the audience. A minor scandal, it is true, but a sensation nevertheless. It is unfortunate that the stage beginnings of Dürrenmatt's career were marked by sensationalism, for the nature of the later critical reception of his plays was thus determined. The scandal arose over Dürrenmatt's treatment of religious material. Dürrenmatt bases the play on a literal interpretation of the Holy Scripture: the last shall be first and the first shall be last. By carrying to a logical extreme what is written in the Bible, and doing so in a scurrilous manner, he achieved a kind of success through sensationalism. The seriousness of the subject matter and the frivolous treatment which it received provided a jarring contrast for an audience that was not used to such a mixture of the sacred and the profane.

If the manner of dealing with historical material was new and strange, many of the techniques were quite familiar. The form of presentation was, in fact, highly unoriginal. The influence of Brecht, to say nothing of Thornton Wilder, is apparent not only in every scene, but also in the whole structure of the loosely constructed "epic" drama. There are also echoes, in both form and content, of older German dramatists. As a historical play about the Anabaptists in Münster the play recalls Goethe's *Götz von Berlichingen* and Gerhart Hauptmann's *Florian Geyer*, but also—and just as strongly—the Viennese folk theater and the farces of Johann Nestroy. The framework of the plot is the siege of Münster under the Anabaptists, a well-known historical setting, with the main outlines provided by history and, in their essential course, unaltered by Dürrenmatt. With some difficulty, one can trace two lines of action throughout the jumbled series of episodes: the career of the sensual and cynical nihilist Bockelson and his struggle

for power with the religious ascetic Knipperdollinck, who takes
the words of the Bible literally and translates them into action;
and the struggle of the city to survive against the forces allied to
besiege and conquer it. The sensualist achieves a temporary triumph, and some splendid orgies ensue; the ascetic sinks into mis-
ery and absurdity, but rejoices in his suffering and his submission
to the Word of God. The careers of the two main figures run parallel rather than tangential to each other, but in the last act they
are united in a fantastic, weirdly macabre dance of death. The
city is conquered by a strange alliance of Protestants and Catholics who take their revenge on the heretics within the city. Dürrenmatt has introduced most of the leading historical figures who
were involved in the struggle, and most of them in a highly caricatured form.[1]

For the period immediately after the war Dürrenmatt's language, which mixed dirty jokes with biblical quotations, did not
constitute the only shock effect. Almost equally upsetting to the
audiences of the time was the use of a narrator, in the best Wilder
tradition, who furnished the public with information about the
play. By having the characters introduce themselves to the audience, Dürrenmatt achieved an "epic" effect that represented a
blend of techniques borrowed from Wilder and Brecht, with
echoes of Nestroy. An alienating effect was achieved by the manner
in which Dürrenmatt obviously played with the play, reminding
the audience that it was viewing a stage play and that the whole
drama amounted to a demonstration of the action in the Brechtian
sense. In this way the play took on the nature of an extended
series of monologues, since the self-presentation of each new actor
on the stage tended to limit the action at any given moment to the
figure on the stage and thus precluded any meaningful interaction
of the characters.

These obviously derivative techniques were combined, however, with a genuinely Dürrenmattian element: the biblical message, "Love thine enemies," is taken literally by Knipperdollinck
and rejected by the Bishop. Here we have a theme which is often
resumed in the later plays, namely the ineffectiveness of the organized church when it is faced with a real moral problem. The
contrast between the literal message and the scurrilous style of
presentation is not the only contrast which underlies the play. The
grotesquerie of a scene such as the one in which the woman seller

of vegetables outshouts the monk signifies the clash of levels which gives the play its particular tone. It also represents a use of contrastive elements on the stage which becomes familiar as one gets to know Dürrenmatt. The monk, who is about to be executed, clamors for justice. He is eventually, and quite inadvertently saved by Knipperdollinck, who comes as a penitent, scattering gold among the crowd on the stage, which turns its back to the execution to scramble for the money. The basic effect of the scene is humorous, but in a diffuse sort of way, since the stage is so crowded, and such disparate things are going on at the same time, that no single line of development is possible in a clear-cut way. This is characteristic of the early Dürrenmatt. The more mature Dürrenmatt will apply this basic technique in a much more sophisticated and therefore more effective form, as in the opening scene of *The Visit*, where in the midst of the laughter at the comic juxtaposition the cry for justice is lost. At this point, Dürrenmatt had already learned not to press his points and to let the laughter die out in realization of the serious point that is being made.

If we refer once more to our definition of the grotesque, we see that the scene just discussed admirably meets the requirements that were set up. In a larger sense the whole play is grotesque, since it takes literally a quotation from the Bible and then proceeds to demonstrate, with equal insistence, both the serious and the comic consequences. The attempt to create a kingdom of heaven on earth ends in excesses, depravity, and sheer nonsense, thereby illustrating a fundamental belief of Dürrenmatt's, namely that what man undertakes to do turns into its opposite by a sure and inevitable process and in spite of good will, pious intentions, and noble idealism. The scurrilous contrasts serve to underline the grotesque quality of the play in such larger settings as the plight of the besieged city, which is set in contrast with the pomp and orgiastic revels of Bockelson. The doom of the city and the tragic fate of its inhabitants, together with the cause they have defended, lose their sting, however, through the comic relief which intrudes into every scene, undercutting more often than underscoring the potential pathos, and frequently removing the action from the realm of reality to one of allegorical play. That the moral or message should be buried in grotesquerie is characteristic of Dürrenmatt; but at times his fantasy runs riot and overshoots the mark. The final scene—the mad dance on the roof—goes too

far in the direction of visual representation, since it renders opti-
cally what should be either suggested by words or indirectly in
symbolic fashion. It is an excess of literalness, for it is so exagger-
atedly macabre that it reduces the final gestures of the main characters to the totally impossible and incredible. By overstepping
the limits, Dürrenmatt robbed himself of a true dramatic climax.

The weakness of the play lies not only in its loose structure and
its embarrassment of riches with regard to scenic effects, but also
in the fact that the potential dramatic conflict of faith and
the demands of reality, or of scriptural doctrine in its literal sense
and the demands of secular living in an imperfect world, has been
baldly presented in jarring scenes, but without a resolution on the
same level as that on which the problem was posed. The ending,
of course, is historical, since the defeat of the Anabaptists was a
fact which Dürrenmatt had to retain.[2] But the problem of living a
faith in its literal sense has not been resolved, and the question of
justice, both human and divine, is treated on a humorous level.
The result of the inconclusive treatment of the basic issues is that
the drama does not satisfy either as spectacle or as a vehicle of
ideas. The bearers of the ideas—and the actors are but little more
—seem to live and act in isolation both from each other and from
the course of events. The loose and causally unconnected sequence of scenes causes the audience to experience each character
as separate and unrelated.

The language of the play is spiced with witticisms, anachronisms, and satiric thrusts, presently mostly in the monologue form.
Even the expected confrontation between Bockelson and Knipperdollinck is not achieved through dialogue. Aside from the direct addresses to the audience, many of the speeches are quasi-
epic descriptions of what is alleged to be happening rather than
integral parts of the action. The Brechtian device of lowering
placards to indicate scenes and breaks in the setting serves to
distract from the thread of action more than it ties together the
disparate and isolated scenes and episodes. On the whole, the
language is not yet entirely Dürrenmatt's own, for derivative elements are still present. There is such an excess of persiflage, exaggeration, allusiveness, and parody that the spectator is easily over-
whelmed by the profusion of the language. Behind the unusual
facets of the style is a readily discernible attempt to break with
conventional theater language. But this negative stance impairs

the effectiveness of the language as a means of communication.

A complete list of the targets of Dürrenmatt's satiric thrusts and parodistic portrayals would be tantamount to retelling most of the play.[3] The Anabaptists are viewed with detachment and depicted in all their foibles; but Catholics and Protestants fare no better. Believers and non-believers are satirized in equal measure; but since everybody and everything is subject to the same satiric distortion, it is hard to determine the main thrust of the play. The comic effects of a person frozen into immobility are exploited in the portrayal of the rigid and statue-like emperor Charles V, in a manner which anticipates the role of the old lady in *The Visit*. But the emperor's role is minor, if not totally superfluous. The comic device of enumeration, present in so many plays and stories of Dürrenmatt, is employed with good effect in the orgies of Bockelson, which prefigure the extravagant menus of later works, notably of *Traps*. There are so many anachronisms, many of them rather obviously planted, that they lose their effect after a while, especially since the audience has been conditioned, from the beginning, to a sense of playing with history.

More valuable for the later development of Dürrenmatt as a dramatist is the fact that in this play his is satirizing a city that tries to create a biblical utopia in accordance with the word of one who said that his kingdom was not of this world. The parody of utopian endeavor is an enduring theme in Dürrenmatt, who firmly believes that all attempts to achieve perfection, as far as the human mind can conceive of it, are doomed to failure. *The Marriage of Mr. Mississippi* and *An Angel Comes to Babylon* are obviously built on this theme, but satire on utopianism is present in nearly all of Dürrenmatt's works, even where it is not the central theme. Even in this first play, the Swiss playwright has already found the appropriate form in which to communicate this fundamental belief of his: namely the farce.

The form of the farce is apposite to a demonstration of the folly of man's striving, and at the same time it frees the author from the restrictions of conventional drama. There are no acts or other larger divisions in the play, and the loose division into scenes is indicated by the use of placards and lighting effects. Dürrenmatt demands a great deal from the stage crew. He later learned to be more modest and to let the text work for him.[4] The external structure of the play amounts to a series of lighting effects bolstered with placards and addresses to the audience which, in their total-ity, are tiresome rather than amusing. Here, as in the language, one feels the polemic attitude toward the conventional form of the drama, without, however, becoming aware that a new form has been created. Even the stage directions—luxurious and lush com-mentaries on the action rather than guidelines for the director—belong to the text of the play more than to the stage representa-tion. But a stand against the traditional drama is not yet a positive achievement, especially when the content of the drama itself sig-nifies a revolt against the problem play. It is also a revolt against its own formal model, namely the Brecht "Lehrstück." But by being a total parody, the play parodies itself to the point of under-cutting its own effectiveness.

A parodistic farce, perhaps on the model of Nestroy, must have some substance and some semblance of progressive action. Dür-renmatt pauses too often for description; he introduces pure nar-rative for its own sake and thereby impedes the progress of the action on stage. A static and narrative impression is left on the spectator in spite of the author's attempts to simulate action. Many of the scenes are entirely independent of the plot and have value only as separate mood pieces; an example is the whole epi-sode about Emperor Charles V, which is extraneous to the action and exists only for its own sake. Such digressions distract the audi-ence from the important themes of the play, which are obscured by the extravagance of the diversions and interrupted by the dis-connected visual effects. Thus the theme of justice—important in every work which Dürrenmatt has written—is ironized and over-laid with comic effects until it is no longer clear or effective. The word justice frequently occurs throughout the play, since the Bishop of Münster, who is aware of the frailty of man and his inability to be just, uses it almost constantly, thereby underscoring the irony of his own failure to achieve it. The Bishop's final speech sums up the meaning of the play: "The sense lies in their tor-ment. For whatever happens manifests Thy infinity, O Lord! The depth of my despair is but a sign of Thy justice and my body lies in this wheel as in a cup which Thou fillest now with Thy grace to the brim!" But in the fantastic setting in which these lines are spoken they remain a lost cry. The mordant irony of the Bishop's acceptance of God's will foreshadows the ending of *The Visit;*

perhaps the most fruitful way to view the play is as practice for greater plays to come.

There are other elements of the play which prefigure more mature utilization of the wealth of inspiration and ideas present in this play. The inglorious and futile death of a protagonist will become typical for Dürrenmatt's tragicomedies. The splendid speech of Knipperdollinck which closes the play is a magnificent statement of faith, but it emerges from a setting that destroys its impact. Knipperdollinck achieves a kind of transfiguration and an ecstatic vision of God's justice and mercy in spite of all appearances, but this possible interpretation of his death is undercut by the bizarre nature of the whole final scene, with its backdrop of a gigantic moon. The moon, however, may also be considered a symbol, though a doubtful one, of the heavens. It may stand for the transcendence which Knipperdollinck sought and Bockelson rejected. But even this is ambiguous and uncertain, for the play has not clearly developed a hero or even an anti-hero. Knipperdollinck and Bockelson follow each other on the stage without having a true confrontation; later, in *An Angel Comes to Babylon*, Nebuchadnezzar and Nimrod will succeed each other without conflict. The play has power and promise, it offers exuberant comedy and suggestions of serious subjects still to come, but it remains, on the whole, inconclusive. His later plays do not end with death on the rack and the destruction of a city; instead they conclude with the ironic triumph of the commonplace, the trivial, and the conventional.

I   The Blind Man

Palamedes: Is God just or unjust?
Suppe: Unjust, my Prince.
Palamedes: Just, my court poet: otherwise the world would not be in hell.

Dürrenmatt's second play is the least well known and the least performed of all his works for the stage. The basis of the play is the contrast between the world as understood by one who is blind and the world as misunderstood by those who can see. Dramatic tension, in so far as there is any, is sustained by the fact that words are used both to conjure up a world that is nonexistent and to falsify the existing world. The basic situation is not that of an apparently ordered society that is thrown into chaos by an outside force—the usual starting point of Dürrenmatt's plays—but rather an illusion of order in the midst of chaos which, in the dénouement, is unmasked as an illusion. True order, and this is a recurring thesis of Dürrenmatt, lies in the human heart and mind, not in external realities, no matter how compelling these may seem to be. The blind nobleman, the central figure of the play, is a type we shall meet in subsequent works, for he is a man who has calmly accepted his fate and triumphs over shallow "realism" through his submission to the brutal truth. At the end of the play, he is justified, even though ruined. The author calls the play "a drama," thus avoiding a commitment to either comedy or tragedy.

Nor is the play a tragicomedy in Guthke's sense. It is not surprising that it is fundamentally an allegory, since the real action of Dürrenmatt's first play had been allegorized and removed from literal action in the theatrical sense. Dürrenmatt clearly meant to correct the obvious errors of It Is Written, which had been rendered abstract and allegorical by the monologues and the parallelism rather than conflict of careers. The play about the Anabaptists is based on riotous spectacle; whereas the play about the blind nobleman during the Thirty Years' War is its antipode, since there is little for the eye, and even the mob scenes are restrained in comparison with those found in its predecessor. In this second play, Dürrenmatt has advanced in technique, for the chief characters confront each other and interact to a degree; but to the extent that the play remains basically allegorical and the demonstration of an abstraction, it fails to create a meaningful dramatic conflict. The stage action is but a pale symbol and a filtered reflection of the meaning behind the action.

As poetry the play is barely adequate; as drama it is too simply calculated in every scene and confines itself so closely to its obtrusive basic message that no engrossing action can unravel on stage. It is successful theater only where it is deliberately funny, as for example in the scene (the play within the play) where the prostitute does homage to the Duke, allowing Dürrenmatt to indulge his love for scurrilous wit. Such scenes function as comic relief, but they also remain foreign bodies within the economy of the play. They are not successfully interwoven with the course of the action and stand out as interruptions. Rhetorical descriptions accompany and gloss the gestures; and the action stems not from dialogue or pantomime, but is a curious blend of gesture and commentary, so that what takes place on stage seems to be a pallid exemplification of the play's basic notion.[5]

"Then touched he their eyes, saying, according to your faith be it unto you" (Matthew 9:29).[6] Dürrenmatt's second play is, like his first, based on the Bible, perhaps too obviously so. It is a version of the Job story, set at the time of the Thirty Years' War, with legendary elements, some crass realism, and some antirealism in the poetic projections of the Duke's imagination. The Italian nobleman Negro da Ponte plays the role of Satan in testing the Duke, who is allegorically Job. But the Duke's faith is stronger than all of da Ponte's wiles and attempts to destroy it; it is also stronger than the deceit practiced by the Duke's son in his attempts to maintain what the son considers to be his father's illusion. The dramatic conflict, insofar as it is realized in the play, consists of the trials of the Duke and his eventual triumph over both the insincere attempts to continue the illusion of peace and prosperity and the efforts of da Ponte to destroy his faith in the divine order.

The plot may be briefly summarized as follows: at the start of the Thirty Years' War, the Duke becomes ill; his property is still intact. When he recovers, he loses his eyesight and continues to believe that his estate is still undamaged, although it has been reduced to ruins. But the Duke accepts with pious gratitude the miracle of his recovery and blesses his blindness for having opened his eyes and for allowing him to see the truth. His son Palamedes, a weak and pale reflection of Hamlet, helps to preserve the illusion that the domains of his father have been spared from the war, but he performs the act of filial piety without love or conviction. The Duke instinctively trusts da Ponte upon the latter's arrival and entrusts all his estate to him as governor. A secondary conflict develops between the son, who tries to defend his father's belief in his sanctuary, and da Ponte, who wishes to destroy it and exult in the cruel disillusionment of the Duke. The father interprets his son's efforts to protect him as mere weakness and selfishness; and although he is quite correct in this belief, the ties that bind father and son are cut. The Duke longs in vain for the love of his daughter Octavia, a rather weak and pale figure, quite unlike the striking and fascinating female figures Dürren-

matt was later to create; but she renounces the world of her father
and brother and gives herself up to da Ponte in the search for a
happiness which she can never attain. In the outcome, the Duke's
faith is stronger than all the forces that assail it, stronger even
than "reality," and even Satan—da Ponte—must admit defeat.
The concluding speeches emphasize the moral of the play:

Duke: Become blind and you shall see.
Da Ponte: I have been conquered by one who will not defend himself.
   For he who opposes me falls prey to me, and whoever resists is lost.
   I leave you now, just as Satan left Job, a black shadow.
Duke: Go forth from me in the name of God.

The Duke preserves his faith in the divine order of the world,
inscrutable to man, which yet possesses a higher meaning and rationale than the world of appearances. On this note of triumphant
faith the play ends. It is unique among Dürrenmatt's dramas, for
it is solely based on the word. "In *The Blind Man* it was my concern to oppose the word to the dramatic location and to set the
word against the setting." [7] The spoken word is used both as a
means of affirming faith in a real and transcendent world and as
an instrument for falsifying the apparent, empirically observable
world. Such great demands on language are made here by the
subtle and often ironic distinctions between truth and apparent
truth, between illusion that is yet a higher reality and an apparent
reality that is illusory, that the play becomes static and takes on
the character of a debate. It is so purely verbal by nature that no
scenery can help to bring action to the stage. With the double
stress on language as the bearer of both truth and falsehood, the
dialogue is overloaded with speculation, forensic elements, and
speeches which move on two levels at once in sustained and
heavy-handed irony.

A strong tendency toward monologue may be observed, especially where one of the main characters sets out to refute a position taken by his opponent. The reply may develop into a lecture
or a detailed exposition of an attitude and thereby become de-
clamatory monologue without any truly dramatic function. Klarmann calls it Dürrenmatt's "most Shakespearean play." [8] The language is highly stylized, full of conceits, antitheses, *double-
entendres*, puns, and allusions. The use of a play within a play to
make the Duke aware of the truth is, of course, reminiscent of
Hamlet; but aside from certain formal features which may have

been derived from Shakespeare, there is nothing to remind one of such a great model.

In addition to the heavy burden laid on language, the setting itself contributes to the difficulties of the play. It is historical, that is, it is placed chronologically during the Thirty Years' War; but the content of the play is timeless and allegorical rather than historical. The play is not truly embedded in time or place, but moves in a world of fantasy and ideas. The result is abstraction, allegory, and a kind of moralizing which is not linked to the historical situation. Since so much depends on the basic contrastive features of the play, namely the discrepancy between what is observable by the audience and what the Duke believes he sees, the demands on the spectator are heavy. The basic conception of the play is too obvious and too openly sustained throughout the play. What might have been effective in a shorter, avowedly lyrical piece palls in the course of this one. The possibilities of varying the basic theme are exhausted before the final moral sermon of the climax is delivered, so that the message, which has been belabored so often, loses its impact at the end.

In retrospect the drama seemed unsatisfactory to Dürrenmatt himself. "The crisis in my career as a writer," he stated, "came after my second play, *The Blind Man*. This play was still mere assertion, the illustration of a religious problem, a piece composed of linguistic arias whose function was hardly indicated. I had avoided creating figures by escaping into the poetic." [9] Dürrenmatt has never again written a poetic drama. It is also significant that this play is one of the few that he has not rewritten or revised. What remains for the student of Dürrenmatt are the themes and the basic intention. The lack of genuine communication and human sympathy is exemplified by the family relations in a way which anticipates *The Visit*. Not even a real community of interest is present, since all the characters are islands without contact with each other. That the contempt for humanity is Satanic is exemplified in the figure of da Ponte, but in a sententious manner that Dürrenmatt avoids in subsequent works. A tendency which we shall observe in his later plays is the rigidly logical illustration of a thesis or position; a basic force, once set in motion, continues until it has taken its worst possible turn. The problem of God's justice and His inscrutable ways with men will continue to remain essential, but the form of presentation will undergo profound changes.

CHAPTER 3

The Masterworks

The dramatist describes people.

I Romulus the Great

EVEN the title of this play, which was Dürrenmatt's first stage success and the first of his plays to enjoy enduring success (in various versions) in the theaters of Germany and abroad, is ironic.[1] It is also his first consistent tragicomedy.[2] The plot is simple and straightforward, as it demonstrates how Romulus, the last Roman emperor, helped bring about the fall of the Roman Empire and worked for its capture by the Germanic hordes. H. F. Garten suggests that one can sketch out the course of the action by considering the last lines of each of the four acts in succession: Act I: Rome has a disgraceful Caesar. Act II: This Caesar must be done away with. Act III: If the Teutons are here, have them come in. Act IV: And thus, gentlemen, the Roman Empire has ceased to exist.

From the beginning Romulus is convinced that the Roman Empire is rotten through and through and richly deserves to be destroyed. His intentions are only gradually revealed to the audience and the other figures of the play. Concurrent with this revelation is the growing awareness, on the part of the spectator, that Romulus is gaining in stature and becoming a figure of grandeur and dignity. The fact that his clowning is only a mask becomes evident only by degrees; and since the audience recognizes his true worth before the other characters of the play do so, a situation of dramatic irony is created. The development from apparent simplicity and folly to impressive moral stature on the part of the protagonist anticipates a similar growth in the character of Ill in *The Visit*. The only other Roman of stature, and the only one whom Romulus takes seriously, is Aemilian. But he is out of tune with the times, suffers as a captive of outmoded ideals, and is the slave of obsolete slogans. The Germanic leader Odoaker is a kindred spirit, who even shares Romulus' hobbies, but he is no longer an effective leader of his warriors.

There are topical allusions and deliberate comical anachronisms in Dürrenmatt's treatment of the Germanic hordes that are about to assume control of the Roman Empire and repeat its mistakes.[3] But it is not they who provide the fundamental contrast with the Roman state, rather it is the true condition of Rome, perceived by Romulus alone, namely the decadence and hollowness which it refuses to recognize. The basic contrast underlying the play is Rome's real condition as distinguished from the ideals it still proclaims and the tradition it pretends to uphold. Romulus seems, at first, to represent this decadence in its finest form, and Dürrenmatt takes advantage of his idiosyncrasies and hobbies for a maximum of comic effect. But the irony displayed in the course of the action consists in the fact that, in the end, Romulus proves to be the last real incarnation of the ancient heroic Roman spirit. In general terms, the plot concerns the discrepancy between fact and fiction in regard to the true condition of the Roman Empire. Dürrenmatt's treatment of this discrepancy marks a new departure for the dramatist. In all subsequent works, the technique of presenting the serious in comic guise will be the hallmark of his style.

There are so many examples of the above technique that we shall select only a typical illustration for comment. The scene in which Rea declaims "tragic" verses from Sophocles illustrates both Dürrenmatt's fondness for parodistic use of the classics as well as the glaring disparity between a fictional emotion, artificially induced, and the real decadence of Rome. With genuinely tragic events crowding in upon the actors, the reading of pathetic lines from a classic, as a rhetorical exercise, creates a humorous effect and, at the same time, conveys a serious message, namely the abuse of literature as a guide for life, the discrepancy between words and feelings, and the insincerity of literary forms of escapism.

The breakdown of a world order and of the ordered world is the theme of the play. The Roman Empire stands here symbolically for Western civilization, and the allusions to the Third Reich are meant to underscore this fact. All but the protagonist suffer from the chaos resulting from this collapse. The supreme irony of the play consists in the fact that it is the emperor who has most effectively worked for the collapse of his own empire, and that he has done all he could to hasten its end. Interwoven with this ironic element in the plot are comic effects produced chiefly by exaggeration, especially in the contrast between the conventional image of a Caesar's proper grandeur and the rustic chaos of Romulus' poultry-cluttered "court." We are used to a cluttered stage from Dürrenmatt's earlier plays. In this play, an organized, carefully calculated action is placed against a background of cackling hens, people rushing in and out, climbing out of clocks, or from under beds, and antique salesmen carrying away the flotsam of an over-ripe empire. In the midst of this confused atmosphere, the mission of a world ruler is parodied in the anti-heroic gestures of Romulus. The posturings of heroism and the clichés of imperial grandeur are the targets of a satire that is sustained farce constantly emphasizing the absurd.

It has already been mentioned that the course of the action gradually reveals the nobility and greatness of Romulus. The collapse of the Roman Empire would not be funny if it were not for the figure of Romulus, who is comic in his rustic poultry yard, but at the same time tragic in his destiny. The conclusion of the play represents the interrelation and interaction of the comic and the tragic in exemplary form. In the "Note" appended to the play, Dürrenmatt remarks that the tragedy of Romulus' life lies in the comic aspects of his end, namely in his being pensioned off and thus robbed of a heroic death. He goes on to assert that his greatness lies in his understanding and wisdom in accepting, with good grace, his departure from the world stage. Romulus is inwardly prepared for death at the hands of the conquering Germanic tribes and, more than that, looks upon his death as the atonement, justification, and natural consequence of his deeds. His belief is that only by the sacrifice of his life can he justify his actions. The tragedy—and the comedy—of his end consists in his being forced to suffer less than a tragic fate. In an ironic way—Dürrenmatt's irony keeps turning, twisting, and shifting its ground—such a banal and humiliating end is consistent with Romulus' deliberately and emphatically non-heroic life, if heroism be understood in the conventional sense. Thus at one level the ending is a comic continuation, with redirected irony, of the earlier humor in the play. But Romulus' heroism has always been of a far higher, subtler order, it being a heroism of the mind and of the will far beyond the comprehension of his compatriots. To deprive him of an end consonant with his inner heroism and the grandeur of his design is, therefore, "tragic."

Two themes which are developed in this play are of great importance for all the later works of Dürrenmatt, namely the problem of justice and the manner of accepting death. The third act is almost entirely devoted to these two themes and prepares the audience for the tragicomic conclusion. Not until this late in the play does it become evident that Romulus has been motivated throughout by his own special concept of justice, in the light of which the paradox of his life becomes clear: to be emperor means to destroy an empire which, he believes, deserves to disappear. The serenity which may take possession of a person who has completely submitted himself to his destiny and who feels at one with his fate is strikingly portrayed in the fourth act. Romulus exclaims: "Never was I more composed, never was I more serene, now that everything is over." We have already encountered this serenity resulting from the full acceptance of fate in the behavior of Knipperdollinck and the blind duke. It is the greatest virtue extolled by Dürrenmatt, and the highest achievement of which, according to him, man is capable. It is the concluding note of "The Tunnel" and is the central theme of several radio plays, notably *Nocturnal Conversation with a Despised Person* and *The Double*. Such a moment of insight, self-realization, and serenity is the climax of *The Visit* and of *The Physicists;* and in his prose, too, Dürrenmatt achieves this supreme moment in several stories— wittily and ironically in "Once a Greek" and rather brutally in "Traps," where the moment of insight is marked by suicide.

The acceptance of fate means an acceptance of one's limitations and of forces that shape our destiny beyond our control or even understanding. With resignation comes a transformation—transfiguration being too pathetic a word and unsuited to Dürrenmatt —and a sense of total adjustment, reintegration, and fulfillment. The clichés of grandeur are silent, and the posturing of heroism (in Romulus' case of anti-heroism) is over. In all of Dürrenmatt's mature works, serenity of soul is typically coupled with the acceptance of death and an insight into the fundamental, if inscrutable, justice of the world order and the rightness of God's universe, including the final judgment of death. Characteristic is the victim's smile of joy in anticipation of final fulfillment. In its first significant use of this state of mind in a Dürrenmatt play, *Romulus the Great,* with its ironic reversal in Romulus' final fate, represents but one variation of what is to become a persistent theme.

The names which Dürrenmatt assigns to his characters are often sources of amusement. Many of them are meant to be both symbolic and humorous. The names of historical persons, such as Romulus, Theodoric, and Zeno, were obviously not invented by the playwright. But his insistence that Zeno is an "Isaurian" may be meant to suggest an echo of some word such as brontosaur or dinosaur.[4] Sulphurides and Phosphoridos are probably meant to suggest Greek fire. Julia is the right name for the wife of Romulus, if an allusion to Shakespeare is intended. The sham and emptiness of the marriage between Romulus-Romeo and Julia are symptomatic of the loss of genuine community in Roman society, as well as being a literary echo. The name Cäsar Rupf is probably funny only to a German-speaking audience which is alerted to the verb "rupfen," which means to pluck, gull, cheat, or fleece. Mares, the war minister, probably derives his name from a combination of Mars and Ares, and is pointedly modeled on Hermann Göring. Tullius Rotundus' name amounts to a hint to the director in charge of casting, while Spurius Titus Mamma speaks for itself.

Much of the slapstick comedy in *Romulus the Great* is visual and forms an essential part of the setting and scenery. The stage directions call for cackling hens and their eggs, for smoke in billowing clouds, and for antics on the part of the actors which lie on a level midway between a cabaret skit and a circus farce. Some of the visual effects on the stage are functional beyond their merely bizarre or amusing qualities, and this represents an advance in stage technique over *It Is Written,* in which comic relief runs riot, and *The Blind Man,* in which the comic interludes are obtrusive interruptions. Romulus eats well, as a civilized man might do; but the loving care bestowed on the menu is a favorite device of Dürrenmatt, who is exorbitantly fond of listing good food and drink. The smoke from the burning archives not only confirms Romulus' skeptical attitude toward Rome's traditions, but also means that future historians will be robbed of much source material—a drastic way of lightening the burden of culture in a Nietzschean manner. The basic setting of the action is functional in all its barnyard absurdity, since it establishes one of the basic contrasts of the play. Some references in the dialogue, however, are erudite in nature, as for example the reference to Domitian as a bad emperor, which is meaningful only if one recalls that he was the first Roman emperor to hire German mercenaries.

The root of all the humor in the play lies in the discrepancy, constantly maintained and reinforced, between fact and fancy, between cliché and reality, between word and deed, between slogan and the true state of affairs. This may be in the form of a discrepancy between a deed and its specific environment which produces comic inappropriateness. From here it is but a short step to Dürrenmatt's fundamental seriousness—nothing is so serious as real humor—for Dürrenmatt is only serious when he is spoofing. Or, to put it differently, it is when we see that he is spoofing that we know he is hiding a serious message. In his mature works he presents his message only in the guise or disguise of wit. This fact may be used as a touchstone to distinguish them from his early, immature prose. In his best writing, Dürrenmatt is thoroughly ironic, in the basic sense of the word. Irony is meant here not as dramatic irony or a special form in any technical sense, such as Romantic irony, but as the expression of meaning by its opposite.

In *Romulus the Great,* there are several minor motifs which recur in other plays by Dürrenmatt: the tendency to climb the façades of buildings rather than using stairs; entrances through grandfather clocks or windows in preference to doors; the love of good food and wine as listed in elaborate menus; a sly, provocative, and playful attitude toward the public and a constant tendency to tease the audience which is more reminiscent of Tieck or Nestroy than Brecht; the institution of marriage as a kind of refined torture for the partners; the wisdom and second sight of old age; the absurdity of people whose minds are enslaved by slogans; scorn and satire directed at bureaucracy in all its manifestations.

Other motifs in a more serious vein, which become fruitful in the later plays, are also present in abundance. The obsession with the destruction of a community anticipates *The Visit.* The concept of justice, both human and divine, in the form of retribution or reward, is central to the play and the motives of its hero. Intimately connected with this is Dürrenmatt's concept of man's capacity for folly and error, but also for redemption, in a world which is basically part of a divinely ordered universe. In *Romulus* the problem of justice is complicated by being embedded in a historical setting and by requiring an examination of the play as an interpretation of man's place in history.

The inhumanity and injustice of those who strive fanatically for abstract justice or for any form of moral rigidity is already familiar to us from *It Is Written*. In his devotion to his ideal, Romulus is a successor of Knipperdollinck and a precursor of the lawyer Mr. Mississippi and the physicist Möbius. Romulus uses his power to help destroy a great empire. His wife and daughter are also accidental victims of the general ruin and chaos. Romulus remains calm in the face of both the national disaster and the personal loss, so that the spectator is tempted to admire his stoic equanimity. "Despite his kindliness in his personal relations with his family and the members of his household, despite his strong sense of personal justice, despite his genuinely felt humanitarian impulses, Romulus suffers from the disease of all morally fervid idealist reformers: he loses the human element when applying his theories. People in the mass are not individualized for Romulus, and so he consigns them to destruction." [5]

The march of history refutes both Romulus and his kindred spirit Odoaker. Romulus is a despot who tries to influence the course of events and interfere with the cosmic order. But one cannot correct history. [6] Does the "moral" of the play, then, consist in teaching resignation and supine yielding to forces which man can neither comprehend nor command? Perhaps man's intelligence counts for nothing, and the virtues which Romulus gradually reveals in the course of the play—his insights, his patience, his urbane wit and wisdom—count for nothing. Perhaps the only value of these virtues lies in the fact that they enable Romulus to act with dignity in a ludicrous situation not of his own making. Both historically and according to the play Romulus neither delayed nor accelerated the march of events. Perhaps at best, reckoning generously, he accelerated the fall of Rome by a few years. But he knows, as does the audience, that Theodoric will be called the "Great" for the wrong reasons, and that history, the record of man's follies, will continue as before. Julia and Rea are dead, Romulus ridiculous, and Odoaker both frustrated and doomed. The fall of Rome means nothing but a small caesura in the tale of man's aberrations, and a sense of futility lies over all that was undertaken in the course of the play. "People who proceed ac-

cording to plan wish to achieve a definite goal. Chance strikes
them hardest when because of chance they achieve the opposite
of their goal." [7]

If we see Romulus only as a member of Dürrenmatt's cast of
fanatics whose sense of abstract justice impairs their sense of human justice, and who are struck down by the force of a fate which
they cannot reckon but seek to manage, we must conclude that
Romulus is a "negative hero." But his positive qualities and his
ability to surrender and accept his fate are traits which represent
the highest virtues in Dürrenmatt's scale of values. Romulus proceeded according to the best possible human judgment and reason. We know that in Dürrenmatt's view of the world these qualities are not sufficient and that the divine order may make man's
wisdom appear like folly. But Romulus was a light in the gather-
ing darkness, and he undertook the noble experiment of living
well in the light of reason. Romulus is thus not only a precursor of
the fanatic Mr. Mississippi, but also of the Don Quixote figure of
Übelohe of the same play.[8] Romulus emerges, therefore, as neither a positive nor a negative hero, but as a tragicomic figure who
engages the spectator's sympathy to the same degree that he deserves condemnation.[9]

Romulus the Great establishes the pattern of the succeeding
plays in many respects. Romulus is a predecessor of the physicist
Möbius, who resembles him even in details. In both cases, some
one else takes over who continues the very madness they tried to
ward off. Romulus is also akin to Ill, the protagonist of *The Visit;*
for the failure of the personal sacrifice is a motif which gives an
unexpected turn to *Romulus, The Visit,* and *The Physicists.* Even
in Dürrenmatt's first play, the Anabaptists, by taking the word of
the Bible too literally, bring about the very opposite of what they
attempt to do. In *Frank V,* Ottilie achieves the very opposite of
what she has striven for, and like Möbius and Romulus she is condemned to live with her frustrated hopes and watch others reap
the harvest she had planned for herself. Even the successful suc-
cessors fall into patterns like the protagonist-losers: in *The Physicists* Fräulein von Zahnd reminds one very much of Claire Zachanassian of *The Visit;* and in her dreams of glory she resembles the
Teutonic figures of *Romulus.* With this first success the essential
Dürrenmatt is suddenly present with most of the fundamental
themes, motifs, and character types clearly developed, so that for

the careful student of this play there is the rewarding pleasure of recognition and rediscovery in the subsequent works.

II   The Marriage of Mr. Mississippi

The facts of marriage are often horrible.

The subtitle of this work is quite simply "A Comedy," although the term tragicomedy would have been quite appropriate.[10] The play is based on the proposition that earth knows no hell like a marriage. However skeptically one may view matrimony and wedded bliss, it is impossible not to feel the impact of the grotesque in the scene in which Mississippi proposes marriage to Anastasia as a means of expiating their common guilt. The public prosecutor Florestan Mississippi has poisoned his wife while Anastasia has poisoned her husband. This is the notion *("Einfall")* which Dürrenmatt employs to set the plot in motion.

The plot itself consists of confused and tangled melodrama deliberately presented out of its temporal and causal sequence.[11] The structure of the play reflects directly the sense of the plot; both are cyclical, and the strange beginning and the expository statements at the end reinforce the sense of eternal recurrence, perhaps too obviously so. The play mockingly starts with its conclusion: after three gentlemen in raincoats and red armbands have shot a fourth man, they disappear. The man just shot to death then arises and addresses the audience to inform it that it has just seen the end of the play, and that the play will now proceed in normal sequence to recount the fate of three men, "who, for different reasons and with different methods, set out either to change the world or save it, and who had the horribly bad luck of meeting a woman who could neither be changed nor saved, because she loved nothing but the moment." [12]

The three men are: Florestan Mississippi, a public prosecutor who is obsessed with the idea of reintroducing the Mosaic law in all its severity (he is a fanatic of justice—an inhumanly rigid and absolute justice intended as a mirror of divine justice, but actually, in this imperfect human world, a caricature of it); Frédéric René Saint-Claude, a professional Communist revolutionary, who is also a fanatic in his insistence on establishing his idea of human justice; and Count Bodo von Übelohe-Zabernsee, a pious doctor who is a fanatic in regard to humility, self-sacrifice, and brotherly love. These three fanatics, allegorically personifing philosophical positions, are each ruined by their relations with Anastasia, a demonic personification of moral nihilism.[13]

The mode of Mississippi's connection with Anastasia is both witty and gruesome, and it serves as a starting point for the play. Übelohe's relation to her must be discovered in a narrative retelling, and it remains tenuous and conversational rather than functional in the plot. The confused lines of the action intersect haphazardly, which would be appropriate for an "absurd" play that has deliberately renounced causality and traditional motivation. But the play retains conventional features and depends on them, so that a hybrid style that is neither convincingly conventional nor consistently absurd results. The monologues of Übelohe contain one "message" of the play, namely that the idealism of a sincere person will always seem ridiculous to his fellow men; but the other "message," that is, the impossibility of reforming the world and reversing the course of history (the lesson of *It Is Written, Romulus,* and *The Physicists*) is developed in chaotic sequence in the careers of Mississippi and St.-Claude. Since Anastasia remains but a feeble link between the two lines of action, the play suffers from an underlying duality without a happy synthesis either of style or message.

The structure of the play is determined by the conflict of the ideas represented by the main characters. All the stage action, with its many interruptions by addresses to the audience, with its placards, deliberately confusing exits and entrances, inverted sequences and calculated impressions of lively chaos, has as its basis the collapse of the ideas presented by the actors in monologue as often as in dialogue. The lush and extravagant stage directions are meant for the reader, not the spectator, and amount to a statement regarding the desired effect rather than a guide to any possible staging.[14] The involved and tangled plot has, of course, a dramatic function: it renders things so complicated that the search for truth and justice seems impossible, and, at the same time, it demonstrates the confusion which results from any and all attempts to establish justice in this world. The plot, the scenery, and the atmosphere created by the interruptions, monologues, and placards are consistent with each other and blend into a unified impression that forms a background for the exposition of ideological positions. Unfortunately, the play is soon reduced to the presentation of philosophical positions. The calculated clutter of the stage and the action presented on it stand in sharp contrast to the simplistic notions of justice proclaimed by the protagonists. The room which serves as the scene of the whole action represents a heterogeneous conglomeration of the claptrap of our culture. In the course of the play, it is gradually destroyed in step with the progressive deterioration of the characters. As their dreams (that is, their attempts at reform) are shattered, the room and its bizarre furniture are also scattered and destroyed.

We have already noted the fact that there are three protagonists, or three standard-bearers of ideas, in the play. They interact only at intervals, since the tendency to use monologue and expository speeches overshadows the dramatic conflict expressed in dialogue or stage action. Übelohe, the mouthpiece of the author, whose statements form the substance of the ideological basis of the play, is not an effective counterpoise to the other main characters. Übelohe does not so much play a role that is interlocked with the action of the drama as the role of a commentator who is almost carelessly linked to the rest of the play. What is typical and significant about him is the fact that, as the one positive character, he is made to appear ridiculous. The revelation of a higher truth in comic form is the hallmark of a dramatist who wishes to avoid pathos and rhetoric and yet desires to convey his serious moral message. Nearly every action and every serious speech in the play is undercut by irony and the shifting perspectives of satire and caricature. At the end, Übelohe appears as the only positively evaluated character, still carrying the banner for a cause that he and we know to be hopeless. His dedication and self-sacrifice have repeatedly been made to appear ludicrous, and his ideal of absolute love and truth has been revealed as illusory. But man's hope lies in what the world considers illusory, as we have learned from *The Blind Man.* Typical is the scene in the middle of the play where Übelohe steps forward to address the audience. What he has to say forms the serious core of the play, yet the manner of presenting it gives it the stamp of a comic interruption.

As in all of Dürrenmatt's plays, the problem of justice is the central theme. From the early plays we know that the emphasis will be on a distortion of justice, a fanatic and exaggerated form of righteousness which will appear ridiculous when its true relation to the cosmic order is revealed. Mr. Mississippi's monomania and moral rigidity are analogous to the spirit of both Knipperdollinck and Romulus, and anticipate the behavior of Claire Zachanassian of *The Visit*. Dürrenmatt prefers to present a parodied view of justice rather than a moralizing poetic justice, and thus achieves his message by indirect means. The personal life of the state attorney forms the first and obvious contrast to his views of abstract justice. The opposite view of justice personified by St.-Claude is, as we have noted, presented more in parallel than by means of a direct conflict. The real basis for comparison is the career of Übelohe, whose life is based on selfless service and altruism. He fails in a worldly sense, but clings to his faith, a Don Quixote who is happy with what to the world must seem a comic illusion. For him the world is

> An eternal comedy
> That illuminates His magnificence
> Nourished by our impotence.[15]

He attains the solace which, in Dürrenmatt's plays, always accompanies this recognition and is its chief reward and compensation for the ridicule of the world.

The language of the play reflects the jargon of the ideologies in conflict. The pomposity of the language often sharply contrasts with the real motives of the people involved. Even more than in *Romulus* Dürrenmatt uses cliché and the jingle of jargon to characterize his figures. We have already noted this characteristic discrepancy between words and motives, but in this play Dürrenmatt reaches new heights with this device. The general impression upon the spectator is one of extravagance: a preposterously inflated atmosphere is created, which helps to reinforce the abstract, symbolic sense of the play. The constant use of hyperbole and of the most grandiloquent word possible in a given context helps to underline the hollowness of the convictions behind the words and the motives half hidden behind the turgid language.[16]

When Mississippi and Anastasia have poisoned each other and Anastasia has persisted even in the face of death to protest her innocence, the plot has come to an end, and the spectator is now aware how the bombastic language and the clichés of social intercourse have combined to reveal all the chief actors as fools who have clung to senseless ideals. Properly understood, the odd title of the off-Broadway production, *Fools Are Passing Through*, is meaningful and suggestive. Übelohe is a "fool," a self-styled Don Quixote who is, however, positively viewed by the author. Idealism will always seem folly to the world; and idealism sustained in the face of repeated defeats must appear doubly foolish. It is also true that the fools are "passing through"—but they will return, since they are eternal, recurrent types. Mississippi's folly will be repeated as surely as Übelohe's.

For all its faults, the play represents a landmark in Dürrenmatt's career. It was the first play to be effectively staged in Germany in Munich under Hans Schweikart's direction. Schweikart's production set the tone for later stagings and helped to establish Dürrenmatt's fame in Germany.[17] From this time on, Dürrenmatt commanded attention with every one of his new productions.

III   An Angel Comes to Babylon

Kurrubi: Yes, my angel.

The polar concepts that frame this play are those of heaven and earth. Within this vast framework, the plot is set in motion by the error of an angel. But the error of an angel is not the same as a human mistake and cannot be judged by earthly standards. The angel is supposed to deliver to earth Kurrubi—a divine being whom God has just created—as a companion for the poorest and most miserable of mortals in the great city of Babylon. The angel's error consists in delivering Kurrubi (the name probably echoes "cherub") to the kind Nebuchadnezzar who has, for the moment, disguised himself as a beggar in order to proceed with his program of outlawing poverty. He and Nimrod, his alternate as king, have organized a state-sponsored program to establish happiness on earth by means of a mammoth welfare state. In such a state begging, of course, is impermissible, and the beggars are supposed to be absorbed into the bureaucracy. But Kurrubi accidentally meets Nebuchadnezzar in his disguise as a beggar, falls in love with him and cannot accept him as king of Babylon. Nor can the king accept her, since he prefers his political power as king to happiness with a divine creature like Kurrubi. He abandons her to the mob, which intends to give her up to the executioner. But she is saved by the beggar Akki, who at the end takes her away to some happy Never-Never-Land.

One of the basic paradoxes of the play—that the king is in fact the poorest of the poor and really the lowliest of mortals—is disclosed by the angel's error. The contrast between Nebuchadnezzar's supposedly exalted position as absolute ruler and his true status as human being is too obvious to sustain a full-length play, even though this contrast is heightened by the relationship to Nimrod, his alter ego and the alternate ruler of Babylon. Dürrenmatt may have felt this inadequacy and therefore proceeded to make the beggar Akki the central figure of the play. Akki is one of the great creations of Dürrenmatt, who endowed him with wit, intelligence, charm and humor, and an unquenchable love of freedom and independence. Akki is a free spirit in a managed world. From the beginning, he appears as a person at one with himself and his lot in life and therefore blessed with that serenity which is the result and reward of complete submission to and love for one's fate. The contrast of his self-assured behavior with the fumbling antics of the bureaucracy supplies much of the humor of the play. There is much satire on the creaking mechanism of a totalitarian government that seeks to improve the world by social reforms imposed from above.[18]

The fun that Dürrenmatt has at the expense of the cumbersome machinery of government remains within the framework of the original contrast between heaven and earth. The more the depths of human frailty are revealed, the greater is the contrast with the joyous wonder of the exploring angel. The order of the city-state is threatened by the arrival of Kurrubi, the pure creature fresh from God's hands. The thin veneer of civilization is ready to peel off at the first contact with a creature as pure and innocent as she. With grandiose and sustained irony, Dürrenmatt shows how in the midst of human striving, the presence of the divine leads to chaos and nearly to revolution. The response of all classes of people to the appearance of the angel and to Kurrubi provide Dürrenmatt with a splendid source of satire. The priestly hierarchy correctly states that the appearance of an angel is the real cause for all the trouble and unrest in Babylon, so that the thesis of the plays appears to be that any form of heavenly intrusion will upset the fragile world of man. Organized religion, always one of the favorite targets of Dürrenmatt's wit, is the first social force to deny the existence of the angel and make a profit from it.

The destruction of an apparently well-ordered community by

the intrusion of an outside force is familiar to us from Dürrenmatt's earlier plays (Bockelson in *It Is Written,* Negro da Ponte in
The Blind Man, the Germanic hordes in *Romulus the Great*). In
his next play, *The Visit,* he will portray the outside force that destroys the order of a community as a rigid and powerful person
with demonic rather than angelic power. In Babylon, the order of
the city is undermined by simplicity, humility, and purity. But it is
the beggar Akki, quite as much as Kurrubi, who is an offense to
the organized state. Akki has found a way of life outside the regi-
mentation of the government, and this, of course, is an unfor-
givable crime. Akki, however, knows how and when to yield to
superior force. In order to survive without compromising his
ideals, he becomes the official executioner, thereby joining a
group with distinguished membership in Dürrenmatt's writings.

The setting of the play in a vague time and place—Babylon is a
mythical symbol, not a historical city—allows Dürrenmatt much
freedom in the use of anachronisms.[19] Some of the cleverest gags
are hidden in the stage directions, which call for such things as an
"Old-Babylonian street light." Parodies of German classical literature abound, perhaps the best being an inverted quotation from
Hölderlin.[20] But Dürrenmatt also pays the price for his rejection
of a specific historical location. The play depends entirely on the
suggestive power of its own self-contained symbolism. As in *The
Blind Man,* the lack of a specific setting involves a tendency to be
allegorical. The fact that recurrent types, and not individual characters, are being portrayed is underlined by the complete interchangeability of Nimrod and Nebuchadnezzar on the throne.
These tendencies are largely offset by the creation of a complete
and convincing stage-world that has its own existence. In this respect, it is one of Dürrenmatt's greatest achievements. The author
has succeeded in presenting the nature of human history in terms
of character types whose strivings have symbolic value. What
might have been merely a fairy-tale motif—namely Kurrubi's love
for Nebuchadnezzar—has been converted into the theme of the
impossibility of selfless, pure love on this imperfect earth. What
might have become another story of an outsider and his revolt
against the social structure, has been fashioned into the triumph
of an independent human spirit.

Dürrenmatt's description of the angel is not specifically religious; rather it is a very free portrayal of a slightly comic agent of

the divine order.[21] His awe and wonder at the splendor and beauty of the earth are used as foils to the mess man has made of his world. The angel is even described as being, in an angelic way of course, rather rigid and pedantic. He fails in his mission, does not comprehend the divine plan, and constantly misunderstands what he observes. The angel asserts naïvely, but from an angelic point of view, that in all his travels he has never seen any unhappiness. He functions as a reinforcement of the message that no one but God comprehends the universe. The angel shares with mortal man the inability to understand God's ways, but he differs from mankind in his humility and in his puzzled, yet not querulous, acceptance of his own limitations. It is comforting to realize that even an angel can misunderstand both heaven and earth. Occasionally the angel speaks for Dürrenmatt, as for example when he remarks that the poorer a man is the more pleasing he is to heaven and the more he reveals the perfection inherent in the Creation. But this is not overdone, and the angel remains one of Dürrenmatt's finest characters.

Such moralizing notes as there are in the play come not so much from the speeches of the angel as from the verses spoken by Akki. Akki's last words have no didactic ring, however, but are an eloquent affirmation of this earth, its possibilities, its beauties and wonders, and express both his and the author's hopes that somewhere a new beginning may be made, "with new promise and with new songs." The play is unusual in having a happy ending. Dürrenmatt's final scenes are usually ambiguous, ironic, or both. To date, the Swiss playwright has been unable to write the promised sequel. The reason seems to lie in the finality of the concluding scene and the sense of hope and promise it conveys. The play is in no sense a fragment, but complete and self-contained. And nothing needs to be added to the final thought that although God's ways may be inscrutable to both men and angels, the possibility of grace and divine miracles is ever present.

Of all of Dürrenmatt's plays *An Angel Comes to Babylon* is the one that comes closest to the fairy tale. The hovering angel, with his breath of the Infinite, the pure and innocent Kurrubi, Akki with his rhymed prose, and the general setting in a wonderland of the remote past all combine to produce an atmosphere of make-believe with much charm and fantasy. The suggestiveness of parallels to our own age is maintained not only by the portrayal of a bureaucratic state with modern, totalitarian ambitions, but also by the anachronisms and allusions scattered throughout the play. Most of Dürrenmatt's favorite themes and devices appear in the course of the play: parodies of classic literature, the figure of a sophisticated executioner, fine foods and wines, the claptrap of civilization and its artifacts, the ineffective and comically flexible views of the theologians, who are completely undone by a visitation from heaven. For all these themes, Dürrenmatt has found a light and cheerful tone. As a stylistic achievement, the play ranks among his very best. It is even possible for the author to slip a parody of Hegel into a speech by the angel, which otherwise is a serious statement of the heavenly perspective and the divine possibilities of creation.[22] Such a combination reveals a sure command of language that was lacking in the more exuberant early plays.

The playwright is even able to show Nebuchadnezzar in a tragicomic light. Nebuchadnezzar, who has striven for perfection, ends by opposing his "justice" to the "injustice" of God. His son is an idiot, his plans are reduced to the absurd, and his only answer is to intensify his efforts. Like Mr. Mississippi, Nebuchadnezzar is striving for an absolute condition impossible on this earth; and his striving is made to appear both noble and serious to a degree. At the same time, it is revealed as unnatural and impossible. Dürrenmatt creates variations and nuances in the balancing of the twofold possibilities, with the accent now on one side, now on the other, continuing the technique developed in the portrayal of Übelohe. *An Angel Comes to Babylon* is the freshest and most charmingly poetic of all his plays to date. It is only regrettable that he has been unable to continue with his plan for a trilogy on the subject.

IV The Visit

Chorus: Nothing is more monstrous than poverty.

Dürrenmatt's fame rests on *The Visit* more than any other work, for it is his best play, the one most frequently and widely performed, the one translated into the most foreign languages, and, of course, the play that established his reputation on this side of the Atlantic. It is a play with so many depth dimensions that only repeated readings and viewings yield the full meaning. It may be, and has been, interpreted from many different points of view. It is the most frequently cited of all his plays, especially as an exemplary tragicomedy.[23] Even the most exhaustive critique cannot raise all the possibilities of interpretation or explore all the lines of suggestibility contained in the play, and the lengthiest commentary cannot provide adequate compensation for the pleasure of new discoveries that can be made by every new reading of the text. It should also be noted that it is the most stageworthy of Dürrenmatt's plays; and its inherent vigor is well demonstrated by the fact that it was a stage success even in the distorting adaptation in which it appeared in New York.[24]

Somewhere in Europe, at the present time, the small and totally impoverished city of Güllen[25] awaits the return of Claire Zachanassian, a former citizen who has become a multimillionaire. The citizens, acting under the leadership of the mayor, hope that she will make a generous donation to her native town and revive its economy. They count on her sentimental ties to her former lover Alfred Ill, who, if successful in obtaining the money—and he is quite confident—will become the new mayor of the town amid the acclaim of his fellow citizens. The first picture of the citizens is one of complete harmony and unity, even though it is the consensus of despair. When Claire first arrives, their hopes soar when she seems ready to renew the cordial relations with Ill and with the townspeople. But their hopes turn to horror and indignation when she declares, at a banquet in her honor, that she has returned for one reason only, that is, to buy justice and to right an ancient wrong. Forty-five years earlier she had named Ill in a paternity suit, but he had denied being the father of her child and had been acquitted, largely because of the false testimony of two witnesses he had bribed. Ill has married for money and in order to obtain a business, while Claire was driven from the town, became a prostitute in Hamburg, and later married the wealthy Zachanassian. She now offers the town one billion dollars in return for the murder of Ill.

The mayor, applauded by the outraged citizens, rejects the offer with scorn. But Claire is sure of the lure and power of her promise and settles down to wait. It soon turns out that she is right in her assumption that the promise of prosperity will be too much for the Gülleners. As she calmly waits, changing husbands now and then, the Gülleners begin to succumb to the lure of the better living that now can be theirs. They continue to profess loyalty to

Ill, but gradually their assurances take on an ominous ring as they
buy on credit and become indebted. Their attitude toward Ill as a
person also changes, and soon they are quite sincere in their right-
eous indignation at his faux-pas of forty-five years ago. They
begin to champion Claire's demand for vengeance as something
quite justified. The deeper they fall into debt, the more they de-
spise him and the greater becomes their collective sense of moral
righteousness.

Ill immediately becomes aware of their shifting attitude. After
trying to get protection from the police, from the Church, and
from the Mayor, he tries to flee, but is unsuccessful. At last he
comes to grips with his guilt, wages his battle with his conscience
in private,[26] and assumes responsibility both for his act and its
consequences. In so doing, he achieves that serenity and sureness
of purpose which we recognize as the certain evidence that he is
at one with his fate. This gives him the strength to reject the
request that he solve the city's dilemma by committing suicide, for
he now sees that the town, too, must consciously assume its guilt
in his death. At a solemn assembly, which is actually a travesty of
a town meeting complete with reporters and widespread publicity
he quietly accepts the judgment of the Gülleners. They murder
him in a mass effort, so that no single person will have to bear the
guilt of having accepted Claire's offer. The play ends in a parody
of a Sophoclean chorus singing the praises of their "benefactress,
who departs with her noble retinue."

Such is the plot in its barest outline. But it is impossible to re-
trace the course of the action without stating the essential themes,
namely the problem of human justice and the destruction of a
community. It is part of the greatness of the play that it combines
and interweaves the two major themes in such a fashion that they
become one. Any analysis of the play, from any point of view,
tends to isolate strands of action or motifs that are, in fact, so well
fused that they are inseparable. The critic can only hope that his
tolerant reader will return to the original text enriched and better
aware of the mastery with which the play has been composed.

The beginning is one of Dürrenmatt's cleverest expositions,
since it combines scenes of hilarious comedy with the facts necessary for an understanding of the initial situation. The opening is
not just good stagecraft and entertainment, however, but it also
introduces the audience to a community. The bedraggled citizens

who appear as the curtain rises represent the town as a social unit, and their nearly choral way of speaking, the interchangeability of their roles, and their uniform opinions and attitudes introduce the spectator to the city as a cohesive social organization. It is not poverty alone that is a great leveler, for Dürrenmatt is consciously portraying representative types, not individuals, and underscores this by assigning no personal names to them. Ill and Claire are the only exceptions to this rule. The opening scene also introduces the force that will set the action in motion and become the power that will destroy the moral order of the town, namely Claire and her billions. The final scene of the play echoes this opening, showing us, once again, a united community, whose solidarity is underlined by its choral responses. Outwardly the city has profited enormously, for its prosperous citizens can now sing the praises of their economic recovery. But the price which they have paid is the murder of Ill, and this guilt is not even present in their consciousness, let alone their consciences.

The stage action unfolding between the opening scene and the final chorus and framed, as we have seen, by demonstrations of civic solidarity, is calculated to show the demonic power of money to pervert justice and undermine the moral fiber of a social organization. As in most of Dürrenmatt's works, the theme of justice is central, and what is shown is the perversion of justice in human terms. The inability of man to cling to his ideals in the face of economic pressure is a central motif in the play. The teacher, representing humanistic learning, is portrayed as a person able to see the evil in Claire's offer, but powerless to act or resist. The minister, representing organized religion, is equally helpless and more despicable because of his fatuous and unctuous advice to Ill. The abuse of religious clichés serves to underscore the deep discrepancy between word and deed which gives the language of the play its special texture. Language is used almost exclusively to conceal thoughts and intentions and veil them with words that are formally correct but palpably insincere. Only Claire speaks the unembroidered truth, and her language, by contrast, appears brutal in its frankness. Civil authority fails all along the line, but it is treated without the acid irony addressed to the teacher and minister, who should know better as intellectual or spiritual leaders. That Ill alone has the courage to find himself and accept his guilt is a characteristic Dürrenmatt touch, for he starts out as the lowli-

est of the low and the most venal person of the community. His
transformation is one of the great features of the play. The fact
that he is made to appear ridiculous and even worthy of contempt
at first and only gradually acquires stature and commands the respect of the audience reminds us of the technique employed in
portraying Romulus.

Like that of Romulus, Ill's fate is, at the very end, put in question again; for just as Romulus is denied the death he expects and
deserves, so Ill is denied any beneficent effects after his death. It is
in the final chorus that the acme of the grotesque is reached, for
here it is demonstrated that Ill's death has been in vain, that the
city has learned nothing from its trials, and that Ill has saved his
own soul without redeeming the community. This in itself would
not be grotesque, but only an expression of the futility of personal
sacrifice and vicarious suffering, if it were not for the fact that
Dürrenmatt is not passing judgment on the Gülleners. It is true
and, in a grotesquely ironic sense, good that the city has become
wealthy and prosperous through Ill's death. The audience realizes
that the city is as rotten in riches as it was in poverty, and their
collective action contains no sense of collective guilt and conceals
a lack of genuine community. But Dürrenmatt is not engaged in
simplistic preaching by advocating the virtues of poverty and con-
demning a high standard of living as a bad thing in itself. The
final scene, with its parody of a Sophoclean chorus, is an absolute
necessity for the structure of the play—the audience must know
that the city has already forgotten the tragedy of Ill, as well as its
own guilt in his death. The ending is, at one and the same time,
ironically conciliatory and a severe indictment of man's weakness.
This combination of elements provides the culmination of the grotesque mixture of effects that is present in every scene and sequence of the dialogue and permeates the whole play from the
arrival of the old lady to the final parodied praise of prosperity.

The restoration of order in the community, presented in grotesque form in the final chorus, also serves to remind the spectator
that the world which he has just seen succumb to the lure of
money is his own world. The directions appended to the play
make it clear that the author wishes it to represent our modern
world, but without commentary and without setting any accents
or emphasis.[27] It should be played with grace and humor or, in a
word, as a comedy. It ends tragically for Ill; but as a play it re-

mains a tragicomedy. It is a truism of dramatic theory that the first condition of tragedy is the greatness of the protagonist. Tragedy is possible only in the conjunction of suffering and strength. The suffering of a person of stature and excellence awakens more admiration than pity, since it elevates the spirit and provides moral enlightenment in the triumph of the spirit over fate. Tragedy is concerned with the greatness of man, comedy with his foibles. It is, therefore, possible to speak of tragedy as being more optimistic than comedy. A fusion of tragic and comic elements which achieves a balance of tendencies is attained in this play as it is in few other tragicomedies. It is the function of the language to preserve both elements. For this reason much of the description of concrete details is quite calm and creates a recognizable environment that is by no means estranged or bizarre. The realistic details of setting and environment, the familiar figures represented by the actors, and the general tone set by the discourse provide a firm basis of easily acceptable "realism," against which the grotesque stands out all the more vividly.

As spectators we are, at times, invited to share the deliberate stage illusion. It is Dürrenmatt's usual way of making pathos and sentimentality bearable by undercutting the scene with irony and gently spoofing the illusion. In this manner Dürrenmatt has his sentimentality and, at the same time, avoids its sticky effects. A classic example of this technique may be observed in the scene in which Claire and Ill revisit the wood which was the scene of their love-making many years ago. Ill immediately becomes sentimental as he recalls their youth, and for once his language is almost lyrical. But by this time the audience knows that Claire is no longer a romantic young girl, but a medical miracle held together by artificial limbs. The "forest" is only there by playful suggestion, because the "trees" are symbolically represented by the four anonymous citizens of the opening scene, and the hammering of a woodpecker is imitated by tapping a key against a pipe bowl. The make-believe is so obvious and the mood to be suggested, but not actually conjured up, so at variance with the true state of affairs that the spectator partakes of the double effect produced by the grotesque contrast, smiling at the pretense, feeling sad at the passage of time and the false sentiment it evokes, and feeling relief when the painful atmosphere of the scene is broken at the end when Ill, to his horror, finds that the hand he is kissing is prosthetic. Dramatic irony of great intensity has been combined with the balancing force of comic relief in such a way that we both experience the pathos of the scene and, at the same time, are prevented from sharing empathetically in it.

Foreshadowings and leitmotifs not only accompany the action, but also direct it. Claire's bizarre retinue includes a coffin, whose significance is patent, and a black panther, whose symbolic value becomes rather obvious when we learn that "black panther" used to be Claire's pet name for Ill. Two eunuchs accompany her, and we soon learn that they are the witnesses bribed by Ill forty-five years ago. They fled the country, but were unable to escape her vengeance; and thus, aside from the grotesque effect of their appearance and speech, they serve as reminders of Claire's power and ruthlessness. As the Gülleners begin to buy on credit and thus slowly succumb to temptation, the new yellow shoes that some citizens wear become a symbol of their growing involvement. When we find Ill's own family buying eagerly on credit, we know that Ill is doomed, for now even the most intimate human social unit, the family, has been undermined. It is also at this point that we begin to appreciate the dignity and self-control of Ill, who does not rebuke his family, but accepts calmly what amounts to a tacit betrayal. His leave-taking from Claire in their final scene together is a masterpiece of the bitter-sweet grotesque. Their farewell is calm and composed, quite routine in tone and gesture, and thus it is all the more striking when Claire promises to build him an expensive mausoleum on Capri, where he will have "a beautiful view."

Claire's promise is grotesque, but at the same time it is sincere. She really wishes to enshrine the man she once loved. Her love and her hate have come to be one. And one can almost possibly feel sympathy for her; for she, too, has reached the end of her life. For years she had lived only with the thought of revenge (which she calls justice when addressing the Gülleners); and now that she is about to attain her lifelong goal, the real content of her life is lost. She is still Ill's victim; and as a person living entirely without love she might, in another context, have deserved pity. Although she is the force that sets the whole play in motion, she herself is, throughout, essentially passive. Her words at the end of the first act, "I'll wait," characterize her stage presence during most of the play. She is rigid and inflexible—one might say immobile—and the comparison with a heathen idol, suggested by the author, is very apt. To the schoolteacher she seems like a Medea or an ancient Greek fury in her single-mindedness and fixity of purpose. But in spite of this, her stage role is a grateful one for aging actresses, partly because her repartee provides the best wit of the play. She has a sense of humor, usually grim to be sure, but in delightful contrast to the insincere clichés of the Gülleners. She speaks the unadorned truth with a gusto that puts to shame the hollow phrases of her conversational partners. Her forthright speech, often both crude and cruel, is one of the major contrastive features of the play. Her monstrous demand for Ill's death as a means of achieving "justice" would be merely incredible hyperbole if it were not for the combination of character elements that make her, for all her deadly monomania, a convincing stage character with a special kind of diabolic charm.

Claire had been heinously wronged, punished by the world, and in many ways driven to become what she was. This is readily understandable; but her desire for revenge has become such a monstrous fixation that it has absorbed all other vital forces in her person and left her an emotional cripple. Dürrenmatt has preferred to leave traces of moral ambiguity both in her position and in that of Ill. There is a conflict between the abstract correctness of her demand for justice and the human and humane realization that forty-five years have passed. Claire has become frozen in an attitude of affective sterility, whereas Ill is still capable of development. He passes from an initial response of fear, leading to the realization that there is no physical escape at the end of Act II, through a dialectic of suffering and intense self-examination that culminates in his decision to accept his guilt.

One of the principal sources of the powerful effect of the play are the choral passages.[28] From the opening scene to the final chorus, Dürrenmatt has used repetition and nearly liturgical language to communicate to the audience the impression of a collective acting out of a social ritual. The speakers of this ritual language are not individualized. They are faceless types representing the community. Their solidarity and common way of thinking are underlined by their ability to finish each other's sentences, by their complete agreement, and by their ability to recite clichés in unison. Sometimes merely bizarre effects are achieved by such speaking in unison, as for example in the first appearance of the two eunuchs. But the power of language to conceal intent is both deadly and amusing, that is, grotesque, in the town meeting at which Ill is killed. The crowd repeats the statements of the mayor as if in a liturgical chant led by a priest. The drastic effect of this grandiose scene is heightened by the fact that the dramatic irony is introduced by the presence of the world press, which does not know the real intent of the Gülleners, whereas the audience and the citizens know that Ill will be killed for the sake of a billion dollars. Dürrenmatt is able to attain even further intensification by the stratagem of having the Gülleners repeat their chant for the press. In the repetition, Ill's spontaneous outcry "My God," which shows that Ill is the only one present who does not fully participate in the ritual, is missing. All that is presented as ritualized, stereotyped, or collective is in one way or another false, hypocritical, or demonic. Ill is the only being of full human stature in the play, but Claire is the central character, and the play is named for her visit.

The world—the community order—into which Claire irrupts is not just economically in bad condition; it is rotten to the core, and its moral level may be assessed from the calculated hypocrisy expressed by everyone, from the mayor and minister on down, while they await the arrival of the benefactress. Claire is quite right in considering the world as a business deal or a market where money can buy everything. No theological concepts are necessary in order to understand the market value of the Gülleners, who are inwardly ready and ripe for the force that does not so much strike them as lead them where they would really like to go. It is more nearly the case that the true ordering of the community is revealed than that a genuine order is destroyed by the visit of the old lady. Especially, the second act with its gradual revelation of the changing attitude of the Gülleners toward Ill, reflects the process of unmasking the true state of the community.

The political and economic aspects of the play need little commentary, since the economic plight of the town is clear enough, insofar as it is frequently presented as an excuse, a rationalization, and finally as a motive power for the collective crime of the city. The political framework represents a parody of democratic freedom, or rather, of the license of democracy in a society solely held together by selfish interests. The mayor, the police, the clergy, the intelligentsia (in the person of the teacher), and the common citi-

zens all succumb in equal measure. Yet they are not presented by
Dürrenmatt as being weaker or any more susceptible to temptation than most ordinary citizens of our contemporary world, since
they are depicted as normal and average citizens of a community
that could be found anywhere in the world today. Just as the morality of Claire's actions is difficult to separate from her whole personality, so the question of the town's guilt is complicated by the
problem of economic determinism. The tendency of the play is to
show man's life as primarily determined by economic forces indifferent to moral values. Man seems to be a slave to economic
conditions, a fact which the mouthing of moral maxims cannot
hide. Toward the end of the play, the audience is ready for
change and improvement, but is greeted by the parodistic final
chorus. In the closing scene, the townspeople appear as much
slaves as they did at the beginning: if at first, they were victims of
poverty they are now the captives of prosperity. Only Ill has
found freedom, and he has attained it only by a withdrawal from
the community into death. The price of his freedom was death in
a grotesque mockery of justice broadcast over an international
network.

The critical responses to this multi-leveled play vary from the
trivially superficial to the excessively erudite. It is a tribute to the
inner wealth of *The Visit* that it can appeal to so many different
viewers and supply the grounds for such disparate interpretations.
One common view is that the play is basically a religious drama.[29]
Ill's acceptance of his guilt and punishment, and his insistence
that the community must also face its guilt, is the point of departure for a consideration of the religious aspects of the play. Ill's
path through suffering to the attainment of serenity in the expec-
tation of death is not only the central action but also the characteristic pattern of a religious drama with obvious parallels to
Christian salvation. It was possible for one critic to state: "*Der
Besuch* is a modern presentation of the Passion story, not only in
part or in grotesque or nihilistic distortion, but in the full sense of
the word."[30] It is true that the Biblical echoes and parallels are
numerous, if sought for, but they are not obtrusive and belong to
the texture of the play as one of several formative elements. The
psychological, economic, and sociological levels of the play are
equally important in any analysis which attempts to reduce (both
in the sense of "restore to original position" and to "impoverish,

diminish") to its constituent parts its finely woven fabric. There is no single, simple message or moral in *The Visit*, but rather a powerful action with a wide range of suggestibility.

V Frank V

Böckmann: There is no crime that has to be committed.

"I do not interpret the world. As a playwright this is not my task. In saying this I do not wish to assert that certain human relationships cannot be interpreted on the basis of *Frank V*. Viewing *Frank V* . . . in the insight may result that a democracy of gangsters is impossible. . . . The imagination of the public is something to be trusted. It will see by itself the basic model of a state in the bank of the Franks, or will recognize a session of Kremlin leaders in the nocturnal meeting of the bank employees." [31] We have quoted from Dürrenmatt's defense of this play both because of the severe attacks from critics and because Dürrenmatt himself has assumed a stubbornly defensive posture with regard to this play and its repeated failures.

The *première* of *Frank V* at the Munich Kammerspiele was accompanied by stormy protests, cheers and boos, and all the public signs of scandal. The critics have been unanimous in their rejection of the play,[32] both in its various stage versions and as a radio play.[33] It is most frequently considered a poor imitation of Brecht's *Three Penny Opera*. The play has the subtitle "The Opera of a Private Bank." It is a strange libretto. The music is presumably intended to serve the same purpose as is served by the Gülleners who pretend to be trees, namely, to poeticize the text. The songs function as a kind of comic relief for the scurrilous central notion of showing a gangster-bank in operation. They are meant to make the play less realistic and emphasize the element of make-believe by creating a distancing effect in respect to a caricatured model of the world.[34]

The songs are, however, given various dramatic functions as well. When they are used as commentary, they provide satisfactory mood and entertainment, but when they attempt to narrate the action they become imperfect substitutes for dialogue. But the songs also belong to a familiar Dürrenmatt tradition, since they also parody the classics, which is exactly the purpose of the declamations from Sophocles in *Romulus* and the quotations from

Hölderlin in *An Angel Comes to Babylon*. There is no play by Dürrenmatt that is free from parody of the classics.[35]

The action of the play consists for the most part in demonstrating the many crimes which the members of the bank commit in order to run their enterprise. The collective which runs the bank is headed by Frank the Fifth, who has inherited both the bank and the manner of conducting its business. Dürrenmatt intended the play to echo a historical play by Shakespeare rather than one by Brecht. In his notes to the Bochum version,[36] he emphasizes the parallels with Shakespeare's dynastic plays. The analogy of the banking firm to an English dynasty, however, is less obvious than the resemblances to Brecht. Much of the humor of the play derives from the contrast between the seriousness and dedication to criminal banking procedure on the one hand and the high-minded language of devotion to lofty ideals on the other. As in all of Dürrenmatt's plays, the dialogue is spiced by the discrepancy between what is said and what is really meant.

This play also contains an interesting variation on one of Dürrenmatt's favorite themes. As the employees of the bank—representing a community of crime—systematically kill each other off, they progressively betray ever greater depths of depravity and an ever more monstrous parody of order. Usually Dürrenmatt describes the impact of some external force on an existing order and uses the grotesque approach as a technique of revealing higher truths that have been obscured by the superficialities of life. But in this opera the seeds of self-destruction are portrayed as being within the organization itself. Greed, fear, lack of trust, and a perverted loyalty to traditional procedure are what make the bank ripe for ruin. The fun consists in the fact that nothing is hidden, and that right from the start the audience is being given an exposé and a view of the activities behind the scenes. The starting point of the play is a parody of order, for the machinations of the gangster-bank do represent an organization, even if a perverted one. At that point in the succession of episodes (which might be called the plot) where no further intensification seems possible, the latest generation of Franks, Frank the Sixth and his sister, steps in and overthrows the previous "order," thereby changing our perspective by a grotesque twist.

This shift in viewpoint occurs when the young Franks, much to the surprise and horror of their parents, appear on the scene and

proceed to operate with cold and deadly efficiency. Their calculated and quite legal ruthlessness makes what has gone before
seem mere play—a gruesome and cruel play, to be sure—but by
contrast the actions of the parents seem like fuzzy and old-fashioned romanticism. The actions of the new generation provide an
unsuspected twist that causes even Ottilie, the female fury of the
play, to wish to repent and reform. In a scene of high comedy and
biting satire, she is denied the chance and is forced to continue
her career of crime even after its justification has been lost.

The president of the state who refuses to accept her confession
and who bids her return to business is a minor figure conceived in
caricature and born in satire. But Dürrenmatt does not portray
character here, as he does in his other plays, but presents a variation on the theme of the vast power of money. In its sharp satiric
thrust at a society which fears economic disorder more than injustice, the scene in which Ottilie's confession is rejected is reminiscent of *The Visit*. At the same time, the scene is also a parodistic
echo of Schiller's *Don Carlos* (V, ix and x), in both structure and
language. The purpose of the parody is to remind the audience of
the cruel and cold justice of Schiller's Grand Inquisitor and thus
gain, by means of contrast, a background for the flabby and flaccid
remarks of the president and the travesty of "justice" which he
pronounces. As a stage figure Ottilie is, to a degree, reminiscent of
Claire Zachanassian, but without possessing the latter's grandeur.

There are other points of comparison to *The Visit*, notably in
the figure of Böckmann, the one character in the play who undergoes a moral development. In an environment of total depravity
and devotion to crime in the name of profit, there is little room for
the finer human feelings. Böckmann has suppressed his moral
sense, has denied himself marriage and children, and has done
this guided by the principle of single-minded service to the bank.
When he discovers that there is no honor among thieves, and that
the Franks have been unwilling to permit the operation that
might have saved his life, he undergoes a change of heart and
longs to confess his sins. But the Franks prevent his confession to
a priest by poisoning him. Böckmann's speech on his deathbed is
the only moral decision made in the entire play. "At any time and
at any moment in our evil lives we could have turned back. There
is no heritage that could not be rejected and there is no crime that
has to be committed." [37] But Frank the Fifth and his wife Ottilie

completely frustrate his conversion, which bears no fruit. The scene showing Böckmann's failure to escape from the kind of life he has lived so long remains an isolated high point in the play without visible influence on the subsequent scenes. Like many other episodes in the play, it exists for itself and is not an integral part of a chain of causality. The plot outline can be retold in its essentials without referring to it.[38]

There are some scenes of good comedy in the play, episodes of a semi-independent nature to be sure, but rather funny in themselves. When the few surviving gangsters assemble with their submachine guns in front of the vault and face each other, all equipped with food for a long siege; when an insurance fraud is planned and lightning actually strikes, leaving the bankers duped and forced to pay; when a mine is salted and sold as allegedly containing uranium, and it turns out that it does have uranium ore. These are all scenes humorous enough in their own right, and it is perhaps superfluous to point out that in all of them the fickle force of fate thwarts the careful calculations of the gangster-bankers. The real difficulty in taking this all seriously, or even comically, is that the figures portrayed are not worthy of either our laughter or our censure. The criminals all long for decency, sentimentally yearn for comfort and security, and are therefore only partly credible as criminals. They are weak and feckless degenerates who are not even able to uphold the corrupt traditions of the bank which they have inherited. The new generation of Franks is much more convincing, if not appealing, for they are brutally serious and efficient and will run the bank without phony ideals or fine phrases. The obvious point is that they are all the more dangerous for being honest and legal. The play amounts to a demonstration of the fact that money isn't funny. This has never been sufficient for either the public or the critics, and the play remains a consistent failure in all its versions.

VI The Physicists

Möbius: What has once been thought cannot be taken back.

The Physicists is not a play about the hydrogen bomb and the final holocaust which it can cause at any time in our lives, but a tightly constructed demonstration, with rigid observance of the three dramatic unities, of the impossibility of escaping the conse-

quences of man's scientific thought. Knowledge is power, and scientific knowledge is dangerous power. Man's ability to destroy the
universe with the results of his thinking is the theme of the play.
For this theme Dürrenmatt chose a classic form of the drama. The
traditional well-made play, with a beginning, a middle, and end
that is usually both climax and resolution of the conflict, is a form
that presupposes, and is especially adapted to, the solution of
problems. Dürrenmatt chooses this form for those plays which
pose a problem, but adds the twist that no final solution is offered
to the public, which is left, at best, with a private, personal solution. Dürrenmatt compares his play to the legend of Oedipus both
because it was Oedipus' own *arete* or splendid intellect that enabled him to answer the riddle of the Sphinx (and it was his
unswerving quest for the truth that led him to learn a tragic
truth), and because it was Oedipus' fate to achieve precisely
what he tried so hard to avoid. Möbius, the central character of
The Physicists, is modeled on Oedipus in both respects, and like
him becomes, against his best intentions, an instrument of error.
He tries to avoid his destiny by making great personal sacrifices,
but every step leads him away from his goal. Even in structure
The Physicists recalls Sophocles' *Oedipus Rex,* since Dürrenmatt's play also gradually reveals the true state of affairs behind
the façade of appearances. When the disclosure is complete, the
play is over.

The larger meaning of the play lies in the demonstration of the
inevitability of Möbius' failure to impose his will on the course of
the world, for no individual can solve the problems of the world
or change the course of history. In this respect, Möbius is akin to
Romulus and also resembles him in the futility of his end. But the
plot, as it develops on the stage, disguises fate in the role of
chance, and chance, in turn, is personified in the psychiatrist, the
mad and crippled Fräulein von Zahnd, who is a literary descendant
of both Claire Zachanassian and Ottilie.[39] The play becomes a
tragicomedy typical for Dürrenmatt, since it clothes the tragic action in comic, fortuitous, and bizarre scenes in a manner familiar
to us from the earlier plays.

Dürrenmatt confines the action to a single day spent in the
lounge of a sanatorium which harbors, among its other patients,
three apparently mad physicists. They are under the psychiatric
care of the hunch-backed Fräulein von Zahnd, the owner of

the sanatorium. In the first half of the play, Möbius, a nuclear physicist who has made discoveries whose effects on mankind he fears, has taken on the mask of insanity to prevent his dangerous theories from being revealed to the world. With him in the insane asylum are two other scientists who also feign madness, one pretending to be Einstein, the other assuming the mask of Newton. They are in fact secret agents of rival political powers who wish to obtain Möbius' secrets. Beutler, pretending to be Newton, later turns out to be a physicist-agent for a Western power; Ernesti, the supposed Einstein, is a physicist working for a Communist country. Möbius' own mask is that of King Solomon, whose commands he claims he is carrying out. Möbius himself is politically neutral and tries to avoid involvement with any political power.

The play opens with the police investigation of the murder of a nurse. It turns out that this is the second nurse who has been killed in the asylum in recent weeks. In the course of the play, a third one is killed. Each of the three scientists kills a nurse because she has fallen in love with him and wishes to marry him. When Möbius kills his nurse because she has seen through his pretended madness and wishes to flee with him, it becomes clear that he prefers a personal crime and its private guilt and suffering to a universal disaster. In the second part of the play, the revelation of the futility of this sacrifice forms the climax of the action. After Möbius has persuaded his fellow inmates to remain in the asylum and help preserve the secret, Fräulein von Zahnd drops her mask and reveals that she has copied Möbius' papers, is in possession of all his data, has already started to exploit them, and is determined to proceed without regard for possible consequences. At this point, it also becomes clear that the psychiatrist is really mad and not just pretending to hear the voice of King Solomon. It turns out that she has planned the murders—crimes which mean that the three scientists can never leave the asylum. In resignation, the three physicists resume their pretended roles, this time for good, since they are doomed to remain in the madhouse. There is no suggestion that they have achieved or redeemed anything by this final gesture or, in fact, by any of their efforts. The curtain falls on a scene of utter futility.

The play is aggressively contemporary and topical in its central thesis and its setting, for the time is now and the place is here among us. On the day the play opened in New York in October,

1964, the hitherto largest Soviet spaceship, carrying a record crew of three, returned safely from the stratosphere. The timing, of course, was accidental, but the coincidence was a fortunate one, for it emphasized the fact that the possibility of total destruction from the sky was no longer a dream but was an ever-present reality. The play needs no scare headlines to make clear that it is a parable of our times and a possible model of our present situation. The intent to reveal the problems and paradoxes of our contemporary situation is underlined by the all-important role assigned to chance; for it turns out that a series of fortuitous events has voided the finest calculations and the most ingenious planning. In a world that can be destroyed by accident or error, it is hard to have faith in planning.

It was a theatrical inspiration to arrange that, at the conclusion of the play, the mad old maid, Fräulein Doktor Mathilde von Zahnd, exploits the discoveries which the physicist Möbius has sacrificed his life, wife, and happiness to keep from the world. The effect of this seemingly abrupt and grimly comical turn is that of the grotesque in its finest form. But the general sense of the play leads inevitably to just some such conclusion, since the action is based, throughout, on the futility of individual action, the conviction that ideas cannot be hidden or revoked, that progress, even if it is progress to ultimate disaster, is inevitable, and that man, that frail creature, is not equal to the task of mastering his own ideas. The last conviction, namely that man is not as large as the thought of which he is capable, and that he falls morally behind his intellectual achievements, is the central concern of the play and is present, once one learns to understand the drama, throughout and not just at the final curtain.

What many critics have failed to recognize is the fact that the comedy of the first act, and the comic effects scattered through the second, are but the background and resonant reflector of the serious elements of the play. In addition they have neglected the pathos, hidden under the buffoonery and cabaret effects of scenes such as that between Möbius and his former family, and therefore have concentrated on the "message" of the play. The satirical basis of this grotesque comedy seems to suggest that all the world is a madhouse and that the mad shall inherit the earth and the fullness thereof. It is understandable that critics, bemused by scenes set in an asylum, have leapt to conclusions about the symbolic meaning of the setting. But the setting in a madhouse is not intended to equate the world with an insane asylum; on the contrary, it is the refuge chosen by Möbius to prevent the world outside from being destroyed. Möbius takes the calculated step of giving up his career, his family, and any hope of personal happiness in order to keep his dreadful knowledge from the world. This decision has been made prior to the opening of the play and is the starting point of the plot, which then proceeds to show the futility of the sacrifice. But one should not overlook the fact that the pathos and personal suffering of Möbius' sacrifice are demonstrated twice on the stage: in the scene of reunion with his former wife and in the scene where he kills his nurse.

It is characteristic of Dürrenmatt to present these scenes without false pathos or sentimental rhetoric and to surround them with comic effects. The scenes in question give us the true measure of the man Möbius, who is not a human computer, but a person who has suffered for his beliefs. Except for the outburst at the end of the family scene, his emotions remain beneath the surface, cool, and understated. The spectator must be alert to the human dimensions of what he says and not lose his awareness of personal loss in the midst of intellectual arguments. "Either we have made a sacrifice or we have committed murder. Either we remain in the madhouse or the world will become one. Either we extinguish ourselves in the memory of men or mankind will be extinguished." [40] When immediately afterwards the three scientists drink a toast to the nurses they have killed, the scene—the most difficult one of the whole play to stage—must be played with genuine solemnity and with no suggestion of irony or mock seriousness, since the action is already dangerously close to the risible. If one does not empathize with Möbius' agony, the emotional impact of the play is slight and it remains at the level of a *drame à thèse*, forceful and eloquent in its arguments, but only in these.

Dürrenmatt has often asserted that in the post-war world nothing depends on one person, no one individual being responsible, irreplaceable, or indispensable. Just as no single figure can represent adequately authority and power, so no single character can be the key figure whose life or death, success or failure, will determine the course of history. Science, like politics, has become teamwork. The collective seems to have replaced the individual as a determining factor in all fields. It is not universally accepted that the scientist is representative of the modern conscience, because his decisions, like those of average citizens, are determined by political powers that are remote, impersonal, and largely invisible.[41] From this it follows that the actions of the scientist do not by themselves assume a symbolic significance beyond those of any other human being. There remains, therefore, only the personal sacrifice of Möbius, a futile sacrifice like that of Romulus or of Ill.

Dürrenmatt's characteristically rich and fanciful stage directions reach their most luxuriant growth in The Physicists. They are largely extraneous to anything seen or noted by the spectator and are, therefore, meant for the reader or possibly some stage designer with baroque inclinations. Totally irrelevant details, including the earlier history of both the institution and the surrounding region, are supplied for no apparent reason except the delight in enumeration. The landscape is said to be "soothing for the nerves," but the whole action takes place in a single room, making the complete and extravagant description of the landscape not only superfluous for any normal theater, but also out of range and focus for the audience, whose attention will always be centered on the room. Even the earlier history of some former inmates, who of course do not appear in the play, is given. It seems as if Dürrenmatt's baroque urges, repressed in order to attain the unities of a strict classic form, had taken their revenge and found an outlet in the stage directions.

Hidden away among the elaborate and unnecessary stage directions, however, is a well-known quotation: "A play among madmen can only be treated in classic form." This is all the explanation needed for Dürrenmatt's turn from the loose structure of his more exuberant earlier plays, although it is also a thesis that has been refuted in practice by Peter Weiss's Marat. Actually Dürrenmatt has not adhered to the classic form as strictly as it might seem, since he first presents the satyr play (Act I), and then the tragedy, thus reversing the classic sequence. Sometimes overlooked in discussions of the "message" of the play is the fact that the subtitle is "A Comedy in Two Acts." The first act is mostly comedy, full of melodramatic scenes and, on the surface at least, not very serious. There is effective dramatic irony in the scene in which the missionary Rose speaks of the "peace of God" that prevails in the asylum, right after which one of the children picks up the lamp cord with which the nurse was strangled. Dürrenmatt is also exploiting the popular superstition that nuclear scientists may all be mad, since the vulgar notion of the "mad scientist" is reinforced by the awareness of the destructive power that has resulted from their research. Dürrenmatt treats the popular view of the scientists ironically by opening the play with remarks like those of the Inspector, who in a way is quite relieved that the murderer is insane and therefore beyond the law. The audience does not discover until much later that the murder was committed for calculated reasons and not as an act of insanity.

At first the audience is permitted no real insight into the meaning of the action, which appears to be an arbitrary sequence of episodes such as might be expected in a madhouse. The true direction of the play emerges gradually and by the force of cumulative suggestion. The end of the scene with Lina, the former wife of Möbius, is deadly serious, but it contains such a wild outburst that its true implications may not be grasped at once. When Möbius speaks with seriousness of King Solomon, a more somber note is struck. His murder of the nurse Monika after they have declared their love for each other leaves the audience with doubts and speculations about the nature of the play and how it is to be interpreted. Yet all along—as becomes evident afterwards—presentiments and forebodings have been scattered through the first act; and in retrospect it is obvious that many anticipatory hints have been dropped. To cite one example of many Monika quotes Fräulein von Zahnd as having admitted that she is actually crazier than Möbius.

The second act begins by echoing the first. Repetition remains Dürrenmatt's favorite device for attaining humorous effects. All three murders take place in the same way, all three bring the Inspector to the asylum, and the possibilities for variations and amusing reversals of roles are practically unlimited. For some time at the beginning of Act II the Inspector and Fräulein von Zahnd converse in such a way that each repeats the lines spoken by the other in Act I. These interposed lines are amusing enough in their own right, but they also serve to indicate the changes that will occur in the second act. Unfortunately, the stage action of the second act is less lively than that of the first. There is a tendency for discussion to displace action and for debate to prevail over progress in plot. The abstract nature of the discussion provokes

the gestures and language of motion, of rituals such as the meal
which the three scientists eat, or the play with the revolvers, the
big, new, ex-convict warders who replace the nurses, and other
attempts to bring life and motion to the stage.

The debate itself, carried out by the three physicists, is essential
to the play, and not, as has been suggested in some reviews, mere
idle talk. The play must deal with the issues under discussion. An
examination of possible attitudes toward technological knowledge
and its deadly power, and a weighing of alternatives are demanded by the problems which the play poses. The major theme
of all of Dürrenmatt's works, namely justice, is treated only indirectly and by implication. In this play, justice is a question of
what to do with the power that stems from scientific knowledge.
The problem was not a new one for Dürrenmatt, who in 1956 had
published a review of Robert Jungk's book *Brighter than a Thou-
sand Suns.*[42]

Jungk's book not only tells the story of the making of the hydrogen bomb, but also records the doubts and pangs of conscience
among the scientists who were responsible for its production. In
his review, Dürrenmatt emphasizes the role of politics and attrib-
utes the building of the bomb to the forces of international politics. He also stresses the fact that no research can be kept secret
for long, and that any thought process known in one country can
soon be repeated in another. He considers the failure of the scientists to consist in their lack of unity and inability to act as a coherent group that could make decisions. "Knowledge was afraid of
power and therefore gave itself up to the [political] powers." [43]
Dürrenmatt concludes that the leading scientists have simply
failed as human beings. He realizes the pressures to which they
were subjected and the force of the temptations to which they
yielded; but this sympathy with their situation leads him to the
concluding, rather bitter remark that it is precisely because everything is so easy to understand in human terms that the story of the
bomb is so demonic.[44]

The ending of the play is open, since the basic problem remains
unsolved in the terms in which it was posed. According to point
three of the famous twenty-one points appended as a commentary
to the play, the course of the action has taken "the worst possible
turn." The dreadful secrets of Möbius are in the hands of a mad
woman. The openness of the ending is in accord with the twenty-

first and final point which Dürrenmatt makes, namely that a play can induce an audience to consider the problems of reality, but cannot force it to find a solution. A play about physicists, Dürrenmatt claims, must be paradoxical. Physics itself is the concern of physicists, but the effects of their research concerns everyone. That which concerns everyone can only be solved by everybody's efforts.[45] Therefore the ending is also symbolic: the physicists resume their masks, representing, once again, classic figures of modern science, and thus inviting the audience to consider the problem as an enduring one which continues beyond the context of the play. Thus it was and ever shall be. In this same spirit, the last point made as a commentary is an appeal to the audience to participate in the problem and to take a stand.

VII Hercules and the Augean Stables: *A Comedy*

Third member of parliament: The manure has risen again.

After the success of *The Physicists,* a receptive public eagerly awaited Dürrenmatt's next play. While the play about the atomic scientists was still making a triumphant tour of Germany, three evenings were devoted to the *première* of *Hercules* in the Schauspielhaus in Zurich. In spite of brilliant staging, the play was not a success with either the public or the critics. Dürrenmatt's attempt to refashion the original radio play for the stage must be considered a failure. But it is an instructive failure that reveals much both about the essential difference between a radio play and a stage play, and about the development of Dürrenmatt as thinker and dramatist in the interval between the versions of the same subject matter.[46]

The play begins with the end of the fourth labor of Hercules, the killing of the wild boar of Mount Erymanthus.[47] According to the legend, Hercules succeeded in capturing it and carried it to Tiryns to present to Eurystheus. On his way to perform this labor he had his famous battle with the Centaurs. But the opening scene shows Hercules and his private secretary Polybius on the top of Mount Olympus with a wild sow. The boar had fallen into a crevice and was lost. With these changes of the well-known legend, Dürrenmatt sets the tone for his free adaptation. The anachronistic presence of a private secretary, who also fills the role of a public relations agent, is no more important than the fact that the play starts with a failure on the part of Hercules. In this first scene Polybius, who also plays the part of an announcer and commentator, advises the public that the play is not going to be realistic, that it is also not going to be didactic in the Brechtian sense, but that it is a poetic play, since poetry has the power to transfigure everything. This is demanding a great deal, since there is much in the play that needs to be poeticized. A sample stage direction reads: "On the stage nothing but the legendary manure." In fifteen loosely connected scenes another failure of Hercules is exemplified. According to legend, Hercules succeeded in cleaning the Augean stables by diverting two rivers. Augeas refused to pay him, under the pretext that Hercules was merely executing the orders of Eurystheus. All this is changed in the play, as it had been in the radio play. Hercules is never allowed to divert the rivers. What we are shown instead are the difficulties and bureaucratic obstacles which he never overcomes, and an extended satire on the dung-ridden civilization of Elis.[48]

Every story has some uniquely adequate form. In the radio version of the legend, Dürrenmatt seems to have found the genre which best conveys the narrative element of the source material. While listening to a radio play, one's imagination is free to respond to the suggestive power of words and conjure up pictures in the mind, constructing one's own scenery in imaginative participation in the text. The presence on the stage of legendary amounts of the fabled manure impedes rather than helps the imagination. There are still traces of the radio play in the stage version, and most of them are felt to be obtrusive. The play becomes more "epic" than dramatic. Polybius narrates much of the action on the stage, fills gaps between episodes, makes comments and dominates the sequence of scenes in a way quite inappropriate to the stage. Other epic elements are gratuitously introduced. The least successful of these is the unnecessarily long scene with Lichas, the anachronistic postman. Here the satire is presented in a long monologue, the witticisms and somewhat forced anachronisms in an address to the audience, and the interpolated vision of Hercules in the shirt of Nessus belongs to a part of the whole cycle of stories about Hercules which has nothing to do with the action of the play.

Such excursions would not detract from the play, and in fact some of them are quite amusing in their own right, if it were not for the fact that the whole play amounts to a curious and unsuccessful mixture of disparate elements. Myth, realistic details (the manure), poetry, parody, digressions, arbitrary sequences of episodes, moralizing scenes and sermons might all have been integrated in some fashion if the play had some clearly central principle of organization. Instead it remains a radio play that has been recast as a moralizing stage show with a philosophical message. The satire of the radio play was amusing and effective, just because the listeners were not made painfully aware that the play was written by a Protestant pastor *manqué*. The humorous commentary of the original is retained in the stage version, but it has lost its impact, since it has been overlaid with didactic speeches. Dürrenmatt intended to poeticize his original version, but the result is not poetry, rather it is candidly preaching.

In several places, the urge to preach has robbed scenes of their wit and humor. In a scene rich with comic possibilities—Augeas is milking the cows among enormous heaps of manure—the angry and frustrated Hercules breaks in to complain bitterly of his conflicts with the many bureaus, committees, subcommittees, and other extravagant outlets of officialdom in Elis. But the scene is not intended to be funny. Augeas quite seriously advises Hercules: "I am the president of this country and have to abide by its laws, and I beg you to do the same. Therefore take up the struggle against bureaucracy as courageously as you fight against monsters. Don't destroy them, persuade them." [49] In the same spirit, Augeas, now quite obviously the mouthpiece of the author, advises his son Phyleus in the final scene: "Have the courage to live here in the midst of this barren and unformed land: that is the Herculean labor which I impose on you." Augeas has just revealed to his son that in the midst of the monstrous amounts of manure he has been able to build a refuge in which a garden flourishes. The urge to poeticize—a euphemism for moralize—even at the risk of creating a grating dissonance with the surrounding text, is evident when Augeas, speaking in lofty, almost biblical language, says: "The divine grace of our world's ever becoming enlightened you cannot achieve by force, but you can create the readiness for it in yourself, so that grace—when it comes—will find in you a clear mirror for its radiance." [50]

Such scenes, with their elevated language and high-minded principles, might be acceptable and effective as contrastive elements in the midst of the manure. But the figure of Hercules himself has undergone changes of a kind that makes the whole play very different in substance from the comic and satiric radio play, to say nothing of the original legend. Hercules has become a philosopher. The radio version contained deliberate anachronisms, and Hercules already had a rather humorously skeptical attitude toward the myth which surrounded him, pursued him, and forced him on to one labor after another. Debts and the necessity of preserving his public image were the motives of the ironized hero of the radio play, but a new degree of self-consciousness has been added which makes Hercules not a comic anachronism but a sentimental philosopher of history. Just how far the emphases have been shifted may be gauged by Hercules' speech as he rejects the amorous advances of the love-sick Iole, the daughter of Augeas.[51] The scene is intended to lend Hercules momentarily the stature of a suffering tragic hero, but it functions as an obvious break in style. In the radio play, the problems of being a mythical hero during one's lifetime were treated humorously, and Hercules' tribulations with his wife and his secretary were treated with wit and humor. Traces of this role are left in the stage version; but they clash with the portrait of a suffering, preaching moralist. Largely owing to this basic dissonance, neither the public nor the critics have been happy with the stage version. Its lack of success established a rhythm of success and failure in Dürrenmatt's career, coming, as it did, after the success of *The Physicists*, with the failure of *Frank V* separating that play from his best play, *The Visit*.

VIII   The Meteor: *A Comedy in Two Acts*

Schwitter: My life was not worth my living it.

Dürrenmatt's most scurrilous and most provocative play was staged in several German theaters within a few weeks of its first performance in Zurich. For whatever critics may have said about *Frank V* and *Hercules*, the theater directors and the public are still drawn to the plays of the most popular dramatist writing in German today. The first German performance took place in Hamburg, the city where Dürrenmatt's *Physicists* had been so successful. In Munich it was staged at the Kammerspiele under the direction of Hans Schweikart, who has staged seven of Dürrenmatt's plays. Critics and reviewers were aghast at first, and the chorus of their responses indicates a wide range of feelings rather than serious analysis. Some took *The Meteor* to be an "intellectual joke against the Church"; some saw in it only the deliberate attempt to shock and marveled at the fact that the cabaret style was not yet dead in the modern drama.[52] The reception by the public at the world *première* in Zurich, where the play was greeted with boos and cheers in very nearly equal measure, has remained symptomatic of the violent dissent with regard to this latest play by Dürrenmatt.

No other play has received so much commentary from the author as *The Meteor*. In addition to publishing "twenty points" in a fashion familiar from *The Physicists,* Dürrenmatt has been at pains to explain the play in every interview he has given since he first conceived of it. As early as the fall of 1964 he reported in an interview: "Its theme is nihilism. The central character is a Nobel Prize winner, who lies at the threshold of mortality but is unable to die. In the desperation of his search for death, he throws off all respect for human laws and sets about the systematic destruction of everything and everyone around him. He becomes the absolute individual; his weapon is truth without mercy. At the end he stands alone, aghast at the realization that he is still alive." [53] This outline needs only a few supplementary remarks in order to become an adequate summary of the play. We should add that Schwitter is resurrected from death twice in the course of the play, and that, at the end, he is indeed spiritually alone while, at the same time, being serenaded by the Salvation Army.

The tight, formal structure of the play—which observes the unities of time, place, and action in exemplary form—and its division into two acts, remind one of *The Physicists*. Both plays are simply called "comedy," although the term tragicomedy would have been equally apt. Both contain highly humorous scenes, which shade off into the grotesque, both have paradoxical basic situations, although placing physicists in a madhouse is more conventional than showing a latter-day Lazarus as a tragicomic lecher. And Schwitter is in a different position from that of the physicists who believe in their physics but fear it. He does not believe in his own death but desires it, and his ultimate failure to achieve it represents—in the language of the "twenty-one points" of *The Physicists*—the worst possible turn the play can take. Schwitter believes in Death, as an absolute or abstraction, or as a possibility for other, luckier people. In the play, he casually causes the deaths of several people. These deaths are not deliberate, calculated murders, committed for an ideal or a cause, as in *The Physicists*, but accidental by-products of Schwitter's total disregard for others. At this point it becomes futile to insist on further parallels with *The Physicists* or indeed with any previous play by Dürrenmatt.

At the same time, *The Meteor* is a compendium of all that is typically Dürrenmatt. The play contains nearly every theme and most of the motifs which have occurred to him. In a way, it also represents a return, in a scurrilous form, to the biblical themes of his first two plays; and in the scandalous treatment of the Lazarus theme it is reminiscent of the grotesque extravaganza of his very first play.

Echoes of previous works may be listed as follows:

(1) The will to shock and provoke both in subject matter and in the treatment of religious beliefs. (2) The striking stage effects achieved by the parodistic use of clichés, especially the clichés of piety. (3) The extreme and bizarre basic situation, reminiscent of the reversal of the Job story in *Once a Greek*. (4) As in *The Visit*, a title which is a dominant, highly suggestive metaphor. A meteor suggests a completely fortuitous event, something brilliant that sweeps in from the sky and disappears. As a symbol of chance and its role in man's life it is inappropriate, however, since Schwitter neither burns luminously nor disappears. The credibility of the metaphor of the meteor as a blind, destructive natural force depends entirely on the devastating effects Schwitter has on the people who happen to encounter him. This means that the play seems to be built upon a whole series of chance encounters. Thus the tightly constructed work tends to have the appearance of resting on a sequence of episodes which illustrate the basic metaphor but which also give the impression of a certain lack of causality in their succession.

(5) Several favorite figures reappear in this drama: the old man in his cups reminds one of *Traps;* the call girl is reminiscent of Chloe of *Once a Greek*. In that same story, Archilochos in his rage is a model for titanism under the influence of alcohol. (6) Moral indifference in the face of death where death is conventional, routine, and expected, or reduced to a formula, is a new theme in Dürrenmatt, but in its use as a sustained motif it is reminiscent of the function of the Duke's blindness, although this anal-

ogy can easily be pressed too far. (7) The classical structure, with two acts taking place within the strict observance of the unities, has already been mentioned. The number of deaths on the stage is remotely like *The Physicists*. But the differences with regard to *The Physicists* are also important, since in *The Meteor* Dürrenmatt has used a different kind of stagecraft, employing pauses, monologues, lack of real contact in dialogue, and shifting perspectives in apparently episodic scenes.

(8) Prostitution, always with Dürrenmatt a favorite outlet for fun and humor, appears here in an ironically favorable light: "You sold flesh for money, that's an honest business." [54] (9) The polemics against moralistic posing, phrase-mongering, and conventional morality which is immoral in essence but accepted by society, are more sustained and intense than in any previous work. But the technique of attacking these targets by means of a rigid logic and an uncompromising insistence on the stark and brutal truth is familiar from his earlier works. (10) The attacks on literature as escapism are reminiscent of the satiric sallies of *Romulus* or *Frank V;* but the tone in *The Meteor* is much more bitter, and the opposition of literature to life is more central to the play. The verbal arts are depicted as the arts of deception; and painting, symbolizing the visual arts, has a whole scene devoted to its denigration.[55] "I surrounded myself with people whom I invented, because I could not get along with real people, for reality cannot be grasped at a desk, Frau Nomsen, it only appears in your blue-tiled underworld." [56]

(11) The exaggerated virility of a literary hero who drinks hard and is successful with women has its early form in the figure of Korbes in the radio play *An Evening in Late Fall.* The differences between Korbes and Schwitter are as revealing as the similarities. Korbes had made a routine out of murder in a highly amusing parody full of wit and grandiose irony, while in *The Meteor* the sense of playfulness is lost: now it is Schwitter's total indifference to the lives and fates of others that causes their death. In *The Meteor* what had once been fun and entertainment has become bitter truth, and the basic situation has been completely reversed. Korbes made literature out of his life, whereas Schwitter is prevented from living by his literature. Even where the text echoes the earlier radio play, both the tone and the sense are different. As Dürrenmatt puts it, "The world wants hard facts, not

invented stories. Documents, not legends. Instruction, not enter-tainment." [57] (12) The importance of chance is expressed even in the title, but the role of coincidence in upsetting a man's life is presented quite differently from the earlier *The Physicists*. What we see on the stage, from the very beginning, is the numbing, confusing effect of chance in the miracle of Schwitter's resurrec-tion and in his stubborn refusal to accept it. In other plays and stories by Dürrenmatt, we are usually first shown the plan, the calculated form of life and the decisions made in the light of some idea. By some stroke of chance these plans are then overthrown and turned into catastrophe. This recurrent design is perhaps easi-est to observe in *The Physicists*. In *The Meteor*, the fortuitous event has occurred when the curtain goes up for the opening scene, and the rest of the play demonstrates the grotesque effects of this original blow of fate.

(13) But chance also strikes again: Schwitter is pronounced dead a second time, and yet he lives on. The grim humor of the play depends to a large extent on this repetition. The humorous effects of repetition have long been known to Dürrenmatt, who has made use of this technique in most of his stories and plays. But in no previous work had the device been used as a basic struc-tural element. (14) The grotesque and tragicomic elements which are inherent in the bizarre basic situation are reinforced by a lan-guage which is scurrilous and brutal in its exploitation of the pos-sibilities presented. But when Schwitter exclaims "I keep resur-recting," the shock effect of the statement is nearly lost because it fits so well the tone of near-blasphemy which dominates the entire work. Gradually, the central event—that is the non-death of Schwitter—becomes mere talk and a subject for speculation, thereby obscuring the principles involved and lessening the impact of statements which, in another context, would be striking.

(15) It is impossible not to think of the final mock Greek chorus of *The Visit* when the Salvation Army serenades the non-dying Schwitter in the final scene. Their singing is sincere, their sentiments are pious, and they are genuinely rejoicing at the mira-cle in their midst. Since their faith is quite unproblematic, they provide the contrast necessary to establish a scene of grandiose grotesquerie, as their pious litany furnishes the counterpoint to Schwitter's vain and fervent pleas for death. (16) Scattered throughout the play are expressions of Dürrenmatt's disgust with

modern technology and its concomitant mechanization of life. His disdain is usually expressed by means of satire, and the extended satire of *Once a Greek* is one of his wittiest and best. In *The Meteor,* however, an almost querulous tone prevails. As we have come to expect from Dürrenmatt, attacks on technology are connected with his traditional view of the economic struggle in the modern world as a debasing one. Some of the satire of *The Visit* derives from this source, but less openly, emphatically and bitterly so. At least one speech by Muheim echoes the confessions of the drunken Traps of the short story by that name.[58]

(17) The luxuriant stage directions of Dürrenmatt's earlier plays are lacking, but the use of stage properties as a means of sharpening the focus on the action reaches perfection. The bed— the central and dominant piece of furniture—and the candles, the lighting effects, the verbally suggested stuffiness of the room, Schwitter's coat, the pictures on the wall are all involved in the action in a way which represents an advance over *The Physicists,* where some of the gestures are not integrated with the action. As in *The Physicists,* the action takes place in one room. Once Schwitter has entered this room, which becomes the symbol of his captivity, he never leaves, since to leave would mean that he had succeeded in escaping into death. Most of those who do leave the room in the course of the play are either already dead or about to die. In this way the room takes on symbolic qualities to such a degree that it becomes a structural part of the play.

(18) The suggestive names are common in Dürrenmatt, although not all of them are equally significant in this play. The name "Schwitter" echoes the German verb to sweat—which is appropriate enough—as well as the word "Zwitter," which means a mongrel or hybrid. The name may also be intended to suggest "Schwyzer," that is, a Swiss. The sound of the name Muheim makes commentary unnecessary. Nyffenschwander is an improbable name, but the author's true intent is not clear. The minister Lutz may derive his name from "lutschen," to suck or lick, or from a dialect form of the word for little. Schlatter suggests "schlottern," which is to say shake, tremble, or dangle. There is no ready explanation for the name of Mrs. Nomsen.

(19) As in *The Visit,* the man least likely to be nominated saint of the year is the one to whom a miracle of grace occurs. But the difference between the figure of Ill and that of Schwitter is

more important than any similarity. Ill achieves freedom of soul through struggle, while Schwitter, an equally improbable candidate for divine grace, is an unbeliever and a cynic. Ill attains moral stature and genuine human dignity, but Schwitter only reaches a despair which he cannot even verbalize, although he is a Nobel Prize winner in literature. Schwitter has become so conditioned to his agnosticism that he refuses to accept the miracle that happens to him even when it is repeated.

(20) Miracles are not uncommon in Dürrenmatt. In *Once a Greek* Archilochos feels that he is the "victim" of a miracle. There are lesser wonders in many of Dürrenmatt's works, but none which compares in its overriding importance with that of *The Meteor*. Dürrenmatt was well aware of the dangers involved in taking a miracle as his central event. As early as 1959, when reviewing a motion picture, he wrote:

Miracles are suited for naive genres, such as the fairy tale, the magic theater, the silent movies. . . . A miracle belongs in the sphere of the "deus ex machina." The question, scandalous in a religious sense, of why God performed this miracle, must be posed in the dramaturgy. One is easily seduced by a miracle into committing a certain amount of cheating in the religious sphere. Therefore a miracle must be intentionally unmotivated, as something inherently beyond comprehension; or else its meaning must be very lucidly worked out, especially when it happens twice.[59]

Dürrenmatt is not an idle scoffer who is merely interested in the blasphemous possibilities inherent in the stage presentation of a miracle. On the contrary, the humorous and scurrilous framework surrounding the miracle makes it all the more emphatic. In the same context, continuing from the above quotation, he wrote: "By its nature, a miracle is generally a test or an opportunity, but in any case an aid to belief or its confirmation." In stories such as *Once a Greek*, the miracle is a test of character; and in *The Meteor* the fundamental ironic inspiration was the notion of presenting the miracle as an impediment to faith.

Most of Dürrenmatt's previous plays were based on two basic paradoxes in human life: the fact that the power—or even the will—to do good and reform the world corrupts the reformer without improving the world, and the final fact of death, which does not merely limit man's life and creativity in a temporal sense, but renders all his acts trivial and transitory. Schwitter's callous and indifferent abuse of his power over others is so emphatically illustrated in every scene that the spectator is immediately reminded of his many precursors among Dürrenmatt's stage figures. Equally obvious, and equally important, is the paradox of death, which is both the culmination of life (and, at most, its confirmation) and the conclusion that erases all achievements and accumulations. Schwitter's non-death fails to fulfill anything, although his presumed death wipes the record of his achievements clean and leaves him isolated and alone with a self which he rejects in disgust. His frenzied and futile attempts to sever his ties with this world—as, for example, his burning of the money—are outward signs of his inner state of separation and despair. Unfortunately, the larger implications of the inability to die one's own proper death are obscured by the emphasis on a strictly personal fate and an individual death. Schwitter does not suggest anything more in his person than what he is: the hollow and weirdly ineffectual shell of a man whose life, in any meaningful sense of the word, already lies behind him.

The difficulty stems from the original conception of the play. A comedy about death requires some representative individual to express it and experience it. But there is no compelling connection between Schwitter's freakish fate and the fact that he is a Nobel Prize winner. Only the fact that he has made his living—and shaped his life—by writing fiction, that is, by inventing things and by becoming accustomed not to believe them, is of any importance or has any function. No attempt is made to demonstrate or suggest how he achieved his fame and reputation. Nothing he says or does during the play even remotely suggests the stature attributed to him. Therefore his failure to die remains a personal one and does not become a miracle of resurrection with symbolic overtones.

Schwitter, although the "negative" hero of a comedy, represents formally a partial reversion to older forms of drama. The tragic hero of classical drama must bear full responsibility for his acts, and that is one reason why he has very nearly disappeared from the stage of today. Modern man feels that he is the plaything of forces far beyond his control and rejects any sense of responsi-

bility. Modern intellectuals have replaced tragedy with accident
and fate with chance, the bomb may go off tomorrow, even
though nobody really wants it to.

With these substitutions, the road to the absurd is open in a
world that seems totally determined, but determined by chance.
Dürrenmatt's problem was to find a sphere or dimension of responsibility in which some aspect of moral decision-making is still
valid and convincing. Nothing can be more intimate and personal
than one's own death; but if one is deprived of that, then no
sphere is left. Dürrenmatt had solved the problem in his earlier
plays—as for example in *The Visit*—in which it was Ill's decision
to assume his guilt in the hope of redeeming his community. The
final chorus demonstrates that he failed. But even if the ultimate
consequences of decisions cannot be foreseen or surveyed, some
restricted sphere of moral responsibility must be established if the
play is not to slide over into a demonstration of the absurdity of
life. Schwitter's own private life—or non-death—is all that is left
to him, and even the range of his life is visibly curtailed in the
course of the play. In comparison with plays such as *The Visit* or
The Physicists, which pose the same dramaturgical problem, *The
Meteor* seems almost a regression; for in the earlier plays the de-
limiting and restriction of the sphere of action allowed nonethe-
less a sense of universal validity. Nowhere in this latest play is
there a sense of reaching out to more significant and broader ranges
of implication or symbolic meaning. Even the ending tends to pull
the play back to the line of minimum suggestiveness rather than
to larger symbolic areas which are potential but unrealized in the
theme.

What the audience sees at the end is Schwitter's despair. The
power of the play and its virtue must be assessed by a consideration of the central notion of a double resurrection. The paradox
of resurrection and faith is the fundamental idea of the play. But
we have preferred, up to now, to speak of Schwitter's "non-dying"
rather than of the miracle of resurrection. The ironic point that
sets the basic idea in motion is the fact that Schwitter does not
believe in the miracle that has happened to him, does not participate in it therefore, and tries to undo it by the force of his lack of
faith. Although this totally negative position seems to be unten-
able, he maintains it throughout the play. From his point of view

there simply is no miracle, there is merely an inexplicable and annoying delay in the death for which he longs.

The seventh point in the commentary the author appended to the play states that the fact of the miracle is a proof of God's existence for believers and a scandal for non-believers. Schwitter is outraged, but for personal reasons and not because of his religious beliefs. In the petulance of his repeated complaints there is annoyance, irritation, and frustration, but no sense at all of the miraculous or religious. As part of the drama, this matter-of-fact attitude of his functions as a fine foil to the excitement of the other figures on the stage. But at the same time Schwitter's own stature is reduced. From the point of view of dramatic technique this remains a problem that Dürrenmatt has not satisfactorily solved. He has produced striking contrast effects, but at the price of diminishing the central figure of the play. What we see on the stage is a succession of scenes illustrating the complete isolation of Schwitter, who has never in his life been able to establish a genuine relationship with anyone else. All his life he has been so egocentric that he has become imprisoned within his own ego, much as he longs to escape from it. Escape and oblivion are what he really wants. His suffering, seen in this light, is a logical extension of his whole way of life; and his inability to cope with the miracle is the climax of a life that has been an offense.[60]

Dürrenmatt considers man to be responsible not only for his life but also for his death. Schwitter had no regard for consequences and no sense of responsibility in his life (this is gruesomely illustrated in the scene with Muheim) and is, therefore, not responsible enough to die. In a religious age, a miracle is a sign of authenticity; in an age of skepticism it is a scandal, an offense to common sense, or an aberration of nature.

The miracle of resurrection may also be considered both as a manifestation of chance and its power to disrupt, and as the "worst possible turn" that a story may take. The effect of the miracle on Schwitter is the unifying strand of the action; but the various responses to the bizarre situation serve as contrasting interpretations. The doctor is shattered by what seems to be a revocation of the laws of nature. Like Schwitter, he cannot accept a religious miracle, which would be no explanation at all; and since he cannot doubt his medical training either, he is ruined by the experience.

The minister, who wants very much to believe but who is plagued
by doubts and seeks a sign, is destroyed by the miracle, too, and
thereby joins his many predecessors in Dürrenmatt's plays, for our
dramatist portrays the clergy only in failure.[61]

The minister is the only figure who appears on the stage with a
genuine crisis of belief, since the painter and Muheim are not
really affected by the fact of Schwitter's resurrection, for they are
concerned only with their own problems which arise from the fact
that Schwitter is still alive. Muheim is an accidental victim of
Schwitter's tendency to fictionalize everything, including his own
autobiography, while the son is concerned only with money and is
indifferent to his father's predicament. The call girl, Schwitter's
last wife, is another of his accidental victims, and her death is on
a level with that of Muheim, with the only nuance that her mistake
was to love someone incapable of love. Only Auguste, the wife of
the painter, takes Schwitter as he is, that is, as very much alive
and lustful. She responds to his masculinity without regard to anything else, whether miraculous or otherwise. Frau Nomsen is not a
victim of Schwitter; rather, he hers, since he loses her at just the
point where it seems as if he had at last established real human
contact with another person. She is totally unaffected by the miracle; this endears her to Schwitter, who believes that he has finally
found a person who is living with the truth of life without illusions.
The hard blow of her death is soon followed by the serenade of the
Salvation Army. For these good people, the resurrection is a simple, easily acceptable fact without intellectual complications;
their sincere, if rather naïve, joy forms an appropriate contrast to
all that has gone before. The varying degrees of participation in
the miracle are wonderfully orchestrated and subtly differenti-
ated.

The varying responses to Schwitter and his condition constitute
the visible action on the stage. It has been suggested that *The
Meteor* is merely a loose sequence of episodes, such that almost
any scene, except perhaps the first and last, could either be cut or
replaced.[62] It is true that one can easily imagine other possible
scenes: with a former collaborator, a daughter-in-law, a lawyer, or
a youthful friend, in the manner of *Der Tor und der Tod.* The
play may be, among other things, a parody of Hofmannsthal's
famous drama. It is true that a first viewing could lead to the
notion that *The Meteor* is basically a dramatic monologue with

interspersed scenes, whose causal connections and temporal sequence are arbitrary and thus at variance with the apparently severely classical structure. But once one has understood the principles of variation and intensification that underlie the play, the question of substituting at random among the possible variations can be dismissed.

Schwitter's life and its consequences—for himself and for others —demand specific reflections in interaction with particular people. We are faced with the same paradox as in *The Physicists,* as the role of chance has been carefully calculated. And, finally, we must not forget that the author has designated the play as a "comedy." It is a comedy of situation that is consistent in its exploitation of a basic situation. It is grotesque in its mixture of the deadly serious and the comic, but that again is typical of Dürrenmatt; for it cannot be too strongly emphasized that he is serious only when spoofing and funniest when he is in earnest. In all his plays, the function of the grotesque is to reveal the essential under the veil of the conventional and to unmask the conventional as false and the pompously important as trivial.

It is this blending of forces and effects that lends Dürrenmatt's plays their characteristic stamp. *The Meteor* differs from his preceding plays only in the fact that there is no culmination in a moment of insight that reveals a higher truth, but rather a reduction to a simple but fundamental fact—the necessity of death. Schwitter is about to attain a higher insight into his life and nondeath when the one person with whom he has established a meaningful rapport, Frau Nomsen, dies and leaves him finally and utterly alone. That is an effective stage ending, but not a resolution of the problem, which extends beyond the last curtain.

In the almost compulsive rigidity with which the basic theme is treated in the successive scenes, in the unswerving insistence on the exploitation of all the negative aspects of the problem, and in the final lack of resolution, *The Meteor* represents a climax in Dürrenmatt's creative career. It is also surely a turning point, since the play is patently a dead end: there is no possibility of further intensification in either technique or subject matter. The problematic life (non-death) of an author is the final expression of a line of development which cannot continue, but which must change and take a new direction.[63] Dürrenmatt's relationship to the public and to the critics will also undoubtedly change, since the "twenty points" and his other public comments represent a maximum effort. Any more intense appeals for understanding and further explications can only be self-defeating.

IX *Summary*

In reviewing the eight plays we have discussed, we find that certain themes emerge as common to all of Dürrenmatt's dramatic productions. Different as the works may seem, they are all related in sharing the same basic concerns: justice and man's inability to achieve it in a world remotely and obscurely part of a divine plan; serenity and peace of soul in the humble acceptance of a necessary but inscrutable fate; the destruction of order in a community; the potential goodness of the world (always in combination with man's unlimited capacity for destroying this goodness); the viciousness of economic ambition; the tendency to act on the basis of slogans instead of humane considerations (the tyranny of abstract ideals over personal relations); satire on bureaucracy and the cumbersome mechanism of government; the tragic or tragicomic results of moral rigidity; and the loneliness and frailty of man in all his relationships. This list is not meant to be exhaustive; and the reader may add to it at will. The themes are obviously serious and profound problems of life in the modern world. The reader must be warned again and again that Dürrenmatt's major concerns are always presented in comic form, that the motifs which set the plots in motion are often hilarious, and that the plays are *comedies* in which primacy must be assigned to the wit and humor of the stagecraft and not to the message or moral.

CHAPTER 4

The Radio Plays

Stage-manager: I have many voices at my disposal, and I may say that they are good voices.

AS a serious art medium, the radio play is much more important in Germany than in America. The *Hörspiel* is a genre that has flourished in Germany since the Second World War, attracting to it some of the best writers of the time. Not only dramatists, but also lyric poets have been attracted to the possibilities of an art form based solely on the spoken word and its power to conjure up whole worlds of feeling and vicarious experience. The radio play has proved to be a very flexible genre. The works belonging to that category may be either lyrical and mood creating; they may be epic and present a narrative in dialogue form; or they may blend dramatic, lyric, and epic elements in any combination desired by the author. By the nature of its medium, however, the genre cannot help but have a formative epic element, since everything depends on acoustic effects that are momentary, and there are no sustaining visual aids. This is often emphasized by the use of a narrator or commentator who holds the successive scenes together by his narration. Hundreds of radio plays in German have been published in book form, and many have been edited for school use by American students of German.[1]

Dürrenmatt's interests in the genre are quite varied. Since the fees paid for a radio play manuscript that is accepted for broadcasting are relatively high, and since acceptance is usually much quicker than for manuscripts submitted to a theater, they represent a significant source of income for the author: "Earning money is a stimulant for the writer."[2] Radio plays contributed a great deal to Dürrenmatt's income before his success on the stage made the writing of a *Hörspiel* a luxury. But he has always been interested in the wide range of possibilities that the genre offers. For the author of *The Blind Man,* turning to a form that depends solely on the suggestive power of the spoken word, aided only by acoustic effects, is not surprising. And the radio play seems especially suitable for satire and parable.[3] "For radio, thanks to the lack of any visual element, is very well able, when attempting fantasy, to achieve the necessary suspension of disbelief. . . . It tempts one, more than the stage does and far more than television, to experiment in modern morality plays or parable plays."[4] In his radio plays Dürrenmatt appears as a moralizing satirist in a more straightforward way than in his stage plays, where the profusion of stage effects and the optical elements may distract the audience and not permit the kind of inward, private experience that is typical of listening to the radio. Parody is also easier to sustain in the shorter, more concentrated form of the radio play. Most of Dürrenmatt's parody is purely verbal, so that the form of the *Hörspiel* is well suited to tendencies we have already observed in his stage plays. The great success of several of his radio plays is due to his confident mastery of the form. So perfectly matched are content and form that when converted to stage plays they have been uniformly unsuccessful.

In his *Writings on the Theater,* Dürrenmatt states: "In a radio play, the world is reduced by abstraction to the level of hearing, and that is its great opportunity and its great weakness. The advantage of the theater as opposed to the radio play, and also the advantage of film and television, is the fact that in them language is achieved not as the direct medium, but as the real highlight. The theater has a greater degree of intensification than the radio play. In the radio play, the world is amputated to the level of hearing and in films to that of seeing."[5] The reduction to purely acoustic effects, whether sound effects from the studio or the human voice, means a greater concentration; and since Dürrenmatt's radio plays share the grotesque elements of his stage plays, the opportunities for humor, wit, and scurrilous effects follow each other more closely. For this reason, his non-didactic *Hörspiele* excel over his stage plays in the rapid pace of the dialogue and the witty repartee.

I The Double

The writer: It is one of my principles to tell only provocative stories.

Dürrenmatt's first radio play is, not surprisingly, based on the Bible, namely Romans 5:12–21 and 4:3.[6] But this time Dürrenmatt is not exploiting the tragicomic possibilities offered by a literal interpretation of the Bible, but rather takes salvation by faith very seriously and makes it the basis of the play. All men share in the guilt of being human, and one man's faith is capable of redeeming all mankind: these two articles of faith are the theme of the play. There are many echoes of the pertinent passages from the Epistle to the Romans in the dialogue of the play. But we find also striking echoes of Kafka's *The Trial*, which obviously supplied such motifs as the shadowy and elusive superior court, the question of guilt and justice, and the apparently blind and fortuitous actions of those responsible for the lives and welfare of the others. As Dürrenmatt's most Kafkaesque play, it is, of course, very much in the style of his early prose. The language and the turns of thought and phrasing are very similar to *The City* with its abstract, moralizing tendencies. The lack of a precise setting in time and place, the typical, faceless characters, and the absence of definable contours in either persons or alleged actions are all characteristics which the play shares with the early prose.[7]

The self-confessed parable is framed by conversations between the "author" and the "director" of the play. The introduction is simply a conversation between them, which replaces the address to the public on the part of a commentator or narrator in a stage play. The basic plot device is that the play is in process of production, or rather, of composition, and that it is being developed as it goes along, with the audience acting as eavesdroppers. Debates between author and director interrupt the process, sometimes for the purpose of correcting a scene just enacted, and sometimes for the sake of additions suggested by the director. This technique, quite tedious when repeated, emphasizes the fact that a thesis is being demonstrated and is consonant with the avowedly didactic nature of the play. There are scattered attempts to make the point that there is an element of "independent narrative," the germ of a story, which tells itself of its own accord, if one just allows it to proceed. The more mature Dürrenmatt never stoops to such devices. The central theme, held loosely together by long narrative sections, in which the author describes what is happening, is the abstract and absolute nature of justice beyond man's ability to comprehend it. All men are guilty by virtue of being human; and they are, as in Kafka, guilty before committing any specific act. But there is in the world an ultimate, if inscrutable, justice, which one can only find by surrendering to one's destiny and achieving that serenity of soul which always accompanies such surrender: "Only he who accepts his injustice finds his justice, and only he who succumbs to it finds his grace." The play remains on the level of exposition without narrative or dramatic force. It has the ring of a sermon, in the form of a radio play on a theme from Kafka.

II   The Case of the Donkey's Shadow

Peleias: Really? I thought Civilization was the name of the new hair style they're wearing in Greece.

This work is Dürrenmatt's one extravagant comedy about justice that is devoid of insistent moralizing and refreshingly free of preaching. The problem of justice in human relations and in man's relation to God remains the single, great theme of all of Dürrenmatt's works, but the ways of treating it vary widely. In this play on a theme by Wieland, Dürrenmatt has chosen to make fun of lawyers and the legal apparatus, using broad satire on man's obsessive litigious urges. The subtitle, "according to Wieland, but not very much so," indicates the freedom with which Dürrenmatt treats his source. The story is based on Wieland's play about the folly of the citizens of Abdera, but with free additions and changes that give it a characteristic stamp. The play is a sustained fantasy, with much low humor, countless puns, and punning anachronisms, and much of the humor is based on bold exaggeration. As an example of the author's ability to show his wit in verbal fireworks, it is one of his best, lightest, and most hilarious. There are political allusions and satirical attacks on politics, abused clichés, and slogans, delightfully hollow rhetoric in defense of causes presented with pathos, a song borrowed from Brecht and, throughout, fun, puns, and bombast. The theme of justice itself is treated lightly and with sustained irony; and in the end the shyster lawyers agree that it is proper that the whole city burns up at the fantastic climax. The construction of the work is well calculated. The spreading of confusion started by the trivial cause is shown, first, in its lateral, then in its vertical extension, until the entire city has destroyed itself in the name of first principles and lofty ideals. The community itself becomes personified and functions as a comic figure of the play. The destruction of a community by its own folly is here the occasion for hilarity; but the ending lacks the tragicomic element which dominates plays like *The Visit*. A holocaust that destroys a ridiculous community is the appropriately hyperbolic outcome of the whole slapstick affair.

III   Nocturnal Conversation with a Despised Person

The executioner: Today it is a matter *only* of trivial truths.

This short radio play for two voices, written in 1951, is a manifesto of Dürrenmatt's credo in such a straightforward, unadorned form that Miss Brock-Sulzer treats it separately and does not consider it along with the other radio plays. In style and message it is a return to the prose of *The City*. In the primacy of the moral message and its insistent didacticism it is reminiscent of *The Double*, although the reduction to two voices implies a more compact form and a stricter concentration on dialogue. The subtitle, "A Course for Contemporaries," underlines the didactic purpose of the dialogue, which deals in abstract form with the problem of justice in a world of power and greed. In this imperfect world, power is everything. There are only two great divisions of mankind: those having power, and their victims. Freedom, equality, virtue, honor, principle are all empty and meaningless terms without content.

But there are some humble truths which are still valid. The executioner and his victim discuss the problems of justice and death up to the point where the victim, assured of his fate, accepts his destiny and dies humbly (almost gratefully) with that serenity of soul and peace of mind which Dürrenmatt has so often portrayed as man's greatest achievement. His acceptance of death means, in the dialectic of the executioner, that he has triumphed in the only way that the spirit can triumph in this world. He is about to die a death that is nobler and worthier than his life and the ideals for which he fought. The irony of the play consists in the fact that the despised person, the assassin sent out by unjust powers, to kill secretly and at night is a philosopher who has gained his deep insights into life from the contemplation of death. In the course of the dialogue, he becomes the teacher and spiritual guide of his victim, leading and teaching him as much by his calm certitude as by the force of his arguments.

The curse of power, its corruptive force at all levels and with regard to all sorts of people, and the system which the struggle for power creates are the topics which the victim discusses with his philosophizing assassin. The dialogue is a philosophical debate in which dramatic elements are almost entirely lacking. But the play contains minor motifs which are typical of Dürrenmatt and which recur in other of his works. Except for such little touches, the play remains the statement of a thesis in dialogue form, the pale exemplification of a message. Humility in death and the acceptance of one's fate even if it is an outrageously unjust one are the weapons of those who do not possess power. The assassin says of those innocent people who have died with humility: "The fact that in the hour of his unjust death one lays aside his pride and fear and even his rights, in order to die the way children die, without cursing the world—that is a victory which is greater than any victory of those who have power."

The triumph of the spirit over rationality and common sense, the triviality of death and the reality of the truth which survives the death of the individual—all these beliefs represent a faith in a divine ordering of the world that is ultimately just. This faith cannot be defended by reason, which it transcends, nor proved by the facts of this world, which it defies. It can only be attested by those whose lives are witness to it; for like many great religious mysteries, the lives of the believers are the proof of its essence.

IV   Stranitzky and the National Hero

The Nation's Hero: The defenders of our fatherland have lost their eyes and legs and I am leprous. And so we all have to suffer.

If an unemployed and crippled war veteran suffers, this fact is not newsworthy. If the nation's hero catches leprosy on the toe of his left foot, it makes headline news and calls for publicity. The contrast in reactions to the distress of the sufferers is the basis for this most Brechtian of Dürrenmatt's plays. In this vein, the songs are used as commentary on the action, but it is especially the cry for social justice that makes this sharply satirical play Brechtian. The silent sufferings of the down-and-out are set in crass contrast to the pampered, publicity-inflated pangs of a playboy. The use of hyperbole to create continuous clashes and contrasts is familiar from Dürrenmatt's other works. The crippled veteran Stranitzky lives in the slums, whereas the fatuous, cliché-mouthing national hero lives in the lap of luxury. Both environments are described by an announcer, a very important voice in the play. Dürrenmatt's ability to describe slum living is subsequently demonstrated in *Once a Greek*, a short story built on a similar contrast in milieu.

There is also another similarity to the above-mentioned short story, since the protagonists in both experience a "miracle" that seems to make their fondest dreams come true.[8] The comparison must not be stressed beyond the fact of the miracle, however, because Stranitzky quite foolishly misinterprets the invitation to have an interview with the nation's hero, and his wishful thinking puts him into a preposterous situation, from which he escapes only by committing suicide. The ending of the play, most of which is kept at the level of more or less playful satire interspersed with wit and good humor, takes a savage turn and becomes grimly grotesque. The story's monstrous ending is all the more effective for being unexpected. The message of social injustice is suddenly presented in all seriousness: the veteran's defiance even in death assumes symbolic proportions, and his raised fist is a harsh but appropriate gesture with which to close the play.

In his book on the technique of the *Hörspiel*, E. K. Fischer frequently cites this play for its exemplary use of radio play techniques.[9] Both the use of accoustic effects, to provide impressions of milieu, and the narrations by the announcer are models of the genre. The shifts from scene to scene, from narration to dialogue, the suggestive use of short commentaries introducing the speakers, and the skill with which group scenes with many voices (always difficult for radio plays) are handled have few if any equals in the now extensive literature of the genre. From a technical point of view, this is Dürrenmatt's finest *Hörspiel*. It also contains many familiar themes and motifs. The names given to the actors range from the comical to the absurd. Mr. Whiteblacke speaks for itself; whereas the name Stranitzky echoes that of Gottfried Keller's famous tailor, Strapinsky, in the story "Kleider machen Leute" ("Clothes Make the Man"). The national hero's name, Baldur von Moeve, echoes the name of the infamous Nazi youth leader, Baldur von Schirach, and there are other suggestions of the Nazi period.

Another familiar device found in the work is the use of quotations from the classics as a substitute for original thoughts. Goethe and Mozart (streets named for Mozart recur with surprising frequency in Dürrenmatt) are the classics chosen, but the function of this device is the same as in his other works, namely to unmask the pious and vapid use of the classics as a means of concealing thought or avoiding it altogether. Last but not least, we should mention the references to America as the land of luxury and sybaritic living. America stands for excessive affluence and conspicuous consumption in many of Dürrenmatt's works, but usually without animosity or bitterness. His point of departure is always Europe and the European conditions he knows. From this coign of vantage he proceeds to the condition of man in our time.

V Hercules and the Augean Stables

Polybios: The truth would have ruined Hercules, a fact which his simple nature could never grasp.

In 1957, the Deutsche Grammophon-Gesellschaft issued the long-playing record No. 43013: Friedrich Dürrenmatt reading his *Hercules and the Augean Stables.* In an abridgment especially prepared for this record, Dürrenmatt reads all the parts, including those of the women. In addition, he penned several sketches as illustrations to the text. Dürrenmatt has made pen drawings for many of his works, and almost all of them are humorous and playful caricatures. The folder containing the text of the abridgment is introduced by a page called "Dürrenmatt on Dürrenmatt." Here the author gives a half-serious, half-humorous résumé of his life and career, noting, in passing, that he wrote the play in just one hundred days in 1954: "The village in which I was born and grew up is not beautiful . . . but the little villages which surround it were genuine Emmental and as if conjured up by Jeremias Gotthelf (and so it still is today). It is a region in which milk is the main product." After speaking modestly of the fact that in life he had achieved only the status of a writer, he goes on to say:

But I have saved from the world of my childhood important things for my present activity: not only the first impression, not only the model for my present-day world, but also the "method" of my art itself. Just as I came to know painting as a craft in the atelier of the village artist —as a wielding of paint brush, charcoal and pen—so writing has become for me today an experimentation with different materials. I struggle with the theater, radio, novels and television, and from my grandfather I know that writing can be a form of struggle.

The struggle which forms the central theme of the radio play is not the labor in the stables, but the complex conflicts with the bureaucracy in King Augeas' land. At the end of *An Angel Comes to Babylon,* Dürrenmatt sketched an outline for a sequel to the play. The last sentence reads: "Everyone is against the tower of Babel and yet it is built." In our radio play, everyone wishes to get rid of the enormous amounts of manure, and yet Hercules is never permitted to do it.

The chief target of the satiric thrusts of the play is the luxuriant growth of committees and commissions that a bureaucracy suffering from hypertrophy can create. The paralysis of an all-embracing bureaucracy bogged down in manure receives a witty and good-humoredly satirical treatment. Organization—always associated if not equated with manure—stifles everything. The play is a parable of man's helplessness in the midst of his own ordering of society. Even a national hero cannot win against committees, which are intended as a symbol of man's inhumanity to man. Hercules fights in vain against these more than protean antagonists which multiply and proliferate like the seven-headed hydra. To make it clear that the satire is directed at Dürrenmatt's native Switzerland, many of the citizens of Elis bear names that are comically Swiss *cum* Greek: Pentheus vom Säuliboden, Kadmos von Käsingen, Aeskulap von Milchiwil, and Kleisthenes vom mittlern Grütt.

The second most important satiric thrust of this playful comedy is directed against the sentimentalization of myths and legends. The play starts with a report by Polybios which makes fun of poets and others who create myths at odds with the facts. But he

goes on to condone a certain amount of fiction, since the unadorned truth is too prosaic to be of use for the imagination of
future generations. Poetic embellishments and exaggerations have
their function in the life of a society, since every society needs
heroes and heroic myths.

The mildly debunking tone of the opening is sustained throughout the play, and the author exploits the basic device of contrasting truth and fiction at every possible turn in the story. Polybios,
Hercules' secretary, keeps on the payroll twenty poets who are
supposed to keep Hercules' public image fresh and exciting, without regard for the truth or trivial details such as facts. Hercules
finds the profession of being a national hero very expensive. He
rushes from one adventure to the other mainly in order to keep
ahead of his creditors, but also, of course, to supply the poets with
new material for their fictions. His exhausting career as a living
legend wears on him, and at one point he exclaims in despair:
"Now I must actually play the role that my poets ascribe to me
and the whole world believes, and that is the most terrible of hu-
miliations." [10] The theme of the incommensurability of life and literature is treated more humorously than seriously and is developed for its comic effects. Twelve years later, in *The Meteor,* the
same theme becomes a deadly serious matter and a source of
Schwitter's suffering.

One episode of the radio play, unfortunately expanded in the
later stage version, has the purpose of reinforcing the comic
aspects of exploitation through propaganda. When Hercules, desperately in need of money, takes a job in the circus under the
aptly named Tantalos, his performance illustrates one of the
major themes of the play, namely the management and exploitation of "cultural products," or what is called in German *"Kultur-
betrieb."* The episode is only loosely connected with the main line
of the plot, but it does serve to show Hercules' enormous strength,
a strength which is both helpless against bureaucracy and easily
diverted into trivial channels. Since culture as an object of com-
merce is one of the important aspects of the play, it is not surprising to find literary satire and sly allusions to the classics in the
text. Again, as in *Romulus,* it is Sophocles who is quoted. That
Dejaneira, the wife of Hercules, should quote Sophocles, is amusing enough in itself; but the purpose of this use of the classics is
the same as in all of Dürrenmatt's other writings.

As befits a satire, the language, is parodistic and saucy. Official jargon and the stilted language of politicians are the chief targets, but clichés from every area of life are echoed and used ironically. Puns, an excess of anachronism, broad allusions to Switzerland and—most of all—comic variations on the verbal derivatives of the key word *Mist* (manure) make up the amusing dialogue.[11] Most of the humor is broad rather than subtle, and an atmosphere of slapstick prevails throughout the play. But the ending contains, in its serious moral, the germ of the later stage version. As in the stage play, Dejaneira is credited with having opened Phyleus' eyes to a world beyond the heaps of manure. And more important, Augeas lectures his son on the path of virtue in a form which anticipates the tone of the stage version. But the moralizing does not dominate the radio play, which remains cheerful entertainment.

VI Operation Vega

Wood: Every time I spoke of ideals in my speech there was thunder.

In *The New York Times* for April 20, 1967, there appeared the following brief notice in the report on the UN: "General Assembly. Committee on Peaceful Uses of Outer Space—Continued discussion of program of work for current year." Thirteen years after the composition of the radio play *Operation Vega*, world events continue along the lines which Dürrenmatt portrays with acid irony. The course of history has, unfortunately, kept this play from becoming dated. Its only optimistic note is the assumption, which the listener must calculate for himself with some quick arithmetic, that there have been no major wars on earth for three hundred and ten years. The action of the radio play is supposed to take place in the year A.D. 2255.

Although there is some comfort in the thought that there have been no total wars since 1945, there is the disturbingly grim fact that the world is still divided into two hostile camps just as it is now: the Communist world and the Western or free world. The activities of both parties have been extended to planetary space. Both sides use the inhospitable planet Venus (the name no longer applies to the goddess of love) as a dumping ground for undesirables. Criminals and those who are politically suspect are sent by both sides into exile on Venus and left there to suffer and die in the savage climate. Although both sides use Venus as a penal colony, both would like to enlist the support of the colonists of Venus in actions against opponents on this earth. This is the anomalous situation which exists at the start of the play.

Very early disturbing foreshadowings and presentiments are heard. During the early dialogues, it turns out that several commissars, both Russian and Western, who had been sent out from the earth, have preferred to stay in the cruel and destructive climate of Venus rather than return. What they have found there is a community of suffering that is a genuine community. The inhabitants of Venus—the outcasts from both camps—have attained an inner ordering of their world as a compensation for a political world order that has totally failed. Technological triumphs have only served to exacerbate the basic political dilemmas and have contributed nothing to solving them. On the contrary, they have helped to intensify and magnify the conflict to cosmic proportions. The absurdity of this escalation and spread to outer space is the theme of the play. Under the inhuman pressures of life in the awful climate of Venus, the colonists have returned to a kind of primitive communal living based on absolute equality and cooperation. They have found within themselves a spiritual strength which more than compensates them for their struggle against a physical environment of total horror.

What they have discovered are the basic, human values that had been obscured or destroyed by the follies of a civilization dedicated to material and technical progress. In the fierce struggle for existence, they have had to give up all the frills and comforts of this earth and return to fundamental problems of sheer survival. In doing so, they have found—or rediscovered—essential human qualities forgotten by the civilization they have left behind on our planet. Under the awful pressures of a cruel environment, they have achieved a way of life based on brotherly love and Christian cooperation. This is precisely the same message which is presented by several postwar descriptions of negative Utopias.[12] One of the representatives of the colony tells the ambassadors from earth: "Venus is huge, and we are small. It is a cruel planet. We must struggle if we wish to live. We cannot afford politics."

The quotation above is typical both for the terseness of its language and for the thesis it states. The turgid clichés and pious statements of grandiose ideals couched in rich, lush prose uttered by the ambassadors from Earth have a mockingly hollow ring. One of the most effective contrasts in the play is that between sonorously pronounced ideals which are betrayed and unnamed ideals which serve as actual guidelines for the life on Venus.

As we have come to expect, the abuse of famous authors is part of the satiric contrast. This time it is T. S. Eliot who is used as a representative of the opiate nature of literature enjoyed only as an embellishment for gracious living. The use of language as a means of concealing one's true intentions, typical of all of Dürrenmatt's plays, is more sustained and more richly developed in this radio play than in most of his other works. The play ends with a satiric thrust at the culture vultures who find solace and comfort in reading T. S. Eliot. Since this comes directly after the false pathos and the hypocritical regrets at having to bomb the penal colonists out of existence, it becomes the sharpest attack on literature as a form of escapism and intellectual cowardice until *The Meteor*.

The ambassadors from Earth are, in principle, opposed to violence and destruction. But the demands of power politics are such that moral considerations must yield; and so, regretfully, they destroy the colonists. Even the possibility that the colonists *might* join the other side is reason enough to annihilate them. The reasoning behind political power and its ruthless disregard for the simplest and most fundamental human considerations are displayed here in the guise of fine words and flourishes. Our life is a life of slogans, placards, ideals not practiced and, in general, an evasion of moral responsibility.[13]

As one of the representatives remarks, it is painful to encounter an ideal in real life. The ambassadors from earth return filled more with envy than with guilt feelings. In its biting satire on a morality which allows political necessity to override any and all humanitarian feelings, this is one of Dürrenmatt's harshest plays. But the lesson is present by implication only, for it is presented by an effective but unobtrusive technique of contrast. The language is restrained in its polemical tone, and all the more effective for its subdued and calculated irony.

Operation Vega is unusual among Dürrenmatt's radio plays for the large extent to which it depends on sound effects. The acoustic background is very important and plays an exceptionally significant role. A favorite device of Dürrenmatt's, familiar from the first

scene of *The Visit,* is the interruption of a pompous and formal
speech of welcome by noises which drown out the rhetoric, leaving only snatches of stereotype phrases hanging in the air. The
fiction that sustains the various episodes and holds them together
is that the narrator has taken down the conversations on a tape
recorder and is playing them back with a running commentary.
This technique of presenting a series of flashbacks of dialogue
with intermediate narrative description is applied with exemplary
skill. Moments of silence and pauses in the dialogue—always
effective techniques of the *Hörspiel* when skillfully used—are frequent forms of punctuation in this play. Dürrenmatt achieves a
powerfully dramatic effect with some of these pauses, as when the
contrast with the roar of the violent storms on Venus is created by
the silence of a voice, conscious of its duplicity and guilt, that can
give no answer. The consciousness of hypocrisy silences the voices
of the ambassadors from Earth at several points, and the decision
to bomb Venus in spite of solemn promises is a silent one. As Bon-
stetten had prophesied, one cannot take back the deed one has
conceived. But the colonists triumph in a Dürrenmatt sense, for
they have attained the serenity and tranquillity of spirit which
comes with the honest and fearless acceptance of their fate. Destruction is made to seem a fitting destiny for a community of
suffering that was, for its life-span, a genuine community.

VII   Traps

The state attorney: Only on the pure base of knowledge is it
     possible to erect the seamless monument of justice.

Every story has a particular form which is uniquely appropriate
to it, and every narrative core can be shaped to fit an arbitrary
genre. In a successful work of literature, form and content are but
two ways of describing the same thing; the way of telling and the
things told have become one, and their identity is the evidence for
the excellence of composition. In the case of *Hercules and the
Augean Stables,* it is clear that the uniquely apposite genre for the
tale to be told was the radio play. The broad, rather plain humor
can be conveyed by the power of verbal suggestion alone better
than it can be represented on the stage. In *Traps* the basic story is
subtle and depends on the contrast of fine and gross effects. What
can be suggested and conjured up by language to which one only

listens differs in degree and kind from that which needs to be read within the larger economy of narrative prose, with its freedom of form and detail. In a radio play the author has only the voices of the actors and the sound effects at his disposal. Subtlety and richly varied nuances are, of course, quite possible to achieve with only these means, but the scope of the possibilities is reduced and the limits narrower than in a freer form. An actor—a voice—cannot indicate emotions by postures or gestures, nor can he suggest his relationship to the other actors except by "talking himself out," and therefore being less subtle. He must tell what he sees and experiences, otherwise the listener cannot imagine the circumstances. Either he or an intrusive narrator is forced to describe and be explicit in a way that makes for a very different effect from that achieved on the printed page.

The radio version of *Traps* is much less subtle and satisfying than the corresponding short story; and this can be illustrated scene by scene. The *Hörspiel* opens with a monologue by Traps which directly and unmistakably shows him as ruthless. Immediately the listener acquires an image of Traps which slants his view of the whole play. In the short story, the fact that Traps is ruthless in business affairs emerges slowly and subtly. The same difference between the direct and sudden revelation and the more gradual and, therefore, more finely shaded emergence of a characteristic may be observed with regard to Traps's erotic interests. The radio play reveals his erotic aggressiveness in the same way as his business attitudes, whereas the short story makes its first reference to this aspect of the traveling salesman in the subordinate clause of a marvelous sentence: Traps considers telephoning his wife, thinks of his children, considers the opportunities for erotic adventures in the rustic town, and comes back to the problem of being away from home. Within one and the same syntactical grouping the cast of mind which Traps possesses is revealed brilliantly and without making the reader prejudge the case.

For a non-thinker like Traps, who is insensitive to the finer moral distinctions, it is quite possible to entertain mutually exclusive notions in rapid succession. The alert reader, subtly forewarned by this sentence, which has unobtrusively characterized Traps, proceeds with growing enjoyment to the series of inadvertent confessions which Traps makes. The short story plants hints and suggestions in the early sections and then continues with a gradual revelation of Traps's character which keeps pace with his growing self-understanding. In the short story Traps's insight into his own true nature culminates in his suicide. In the radio play, he awakens in the morning to consider everything that has gone before as a dream; and he drives off with a monologue that echoes the opening of the play. He has learned nothing by his extraordinary experience; it is merely a matter of his having been tested and found wanting.

The basic narrative element common to both versions is the tale of a typical citizen of our time who has an unusual adventure owing to an automobile accident. Thanks to this adventure, which consists of submitting to a mock trial, he achieves an understanding of his way of life. The German title, "Die Panne," suggests a mechanical breakdown. In the short story, but less so in the radio version, a moral breakdown is also suggested. It is emphasized that Traps is an average citizen of our civilization, no better and no worse than others who are engaged in the struggle for prosperity. In both versions, it is indirectly suggested, as in so many of Dürrenmatt's works, that the economic side of man's life is in and of itself evil; and by a series of parallelisms Dürrenmatt even seems to equate business with murder.

As in *The Visit*, the coercive power of economic considerations always overrides the other forces of society. The struggle for economic survival, like that for political power, knows no mercy and in practice recognizes no moral concerns. Man's morals are mere embellishments, or an idle ornamentation of conversation, and they are revealed as meaningless as soon as they come into conflict with economic "needs." Traps is, therefore, no more immoral or less ethically sensitive than the system demands. He has been successful in business by being ruthless, although no more so than others, and he is proud of being a self-made man. By chance he stumbles into the company of retired lawyers and judges, who entertain him by giving him a Lucullan feast, and at the same time—as a form of harmless entertainment—stage a trial.

Traps, as the defendant in the trial, asserts his innocence quite sincerely. It is the claim of the prosecution, however, that every mortal is guilty of something; and the course of the trial proves this admirably, for Traps, quite without realizing it and with unconscious intent, has murdered his boss and rival. In the midst of the orgy of eating and drinking—Dürrenmatt gives us the menu in detail with great relish—Traps is exhilarated by the discovery that he has done something interesting and important. In his growing self-recognition, he becomes euphoric, feels a new sense of his own identity, and welcomes the discovery of his crime. His admission of guilt is the cause of great joy and hilarity for the tipsy old men who are staging the mock trial. Justice and the process of discovering it are presented as something that should be jolly and not terrible or menacing.

Truth and justice as moral matters transcending the paragraphs of any law code are revealed in the midst of an orgiastic and fantastic party, thus fulfilling the requirements for the grotesque in the pregnant sense. In an introductory section to the short story, Dürrenmatt considers the difficulties in the path of a writer who wishes to write "stories that are still possible, stories for writers." After rejecting the possibility of mere personal confession, as well as stories which deal with psychological or medical problems, he suggests that perhaps out of humdrum everyday life, out of all the trivial paraphernalia of modern living with its absence of God, justice, and fate, there may emerge some stories, that is, when humanity appears in an average face, and justice becomes visible, perhaps even divine grace, caught by chance and reflected by the monocle of a drunken man.[14]

The indirect revelation of a hidden but important truth in the midst of comic hilarity is the essence of the grotesque as it appears in Dürrenmatt's works. In this respect, the short story *Traps* is exemplary. The role assigned to chance also marks it as typical of the author, who prefers to arrange accidents and coincidences to set his plots in motion, thereby avoiding pathetic or—in his terms —obsolete devices such as fate. Another feature which the story shares with other prose works by Dürrenmatt is the atmosphere of the fairy tale. Several times Traps exclaims that he feels as if he were acting out a fairy tale. The device of a "trial by miracle" is also familiar from many other works. In the short story, Traps's acceptance of his guilt and the joy and relief he feels are reminiscent of Ill in *The Visit* and many others who find peace both in self-discovery and in the acceptance of their destiny. As the reader has, by now, come to expect, the names of the figures in the story are suggestive and comical. "Traps" may have been derived from "trapsen," which means to stumble or stagger, and it may also suggest "der Taps," an awkward fellow. The prosecutor is called "wrath" and the defender "grief." Gygax seems to echo a trade name, but it may also be a combination of "Gigant" (giant) and Ajax. Dürrenmatt indulges his love for hyperbole in this story in his loving and yet bizarre descriptions of the strange old men and their antics, but the core of the story remains psychologically realistic. The successful combination of disparate stylistic and narrative elements makes it one of Dürrenmatt's finest achievements.

VIII   An Evening in Late Fall

Korbes: You have given me the idea for a radio play, and now you must die, because I only write what I experience, because I have no imagination, because I can write *only* what I experience.

This prize-winning radio play is one of Dürrenmatt's most delightful and witty satires. It is intended as a spoof of the hardboiled school of confessional writing, with many obvious allusions to Hemingway and a parodied way of "living one's literature." The central figure, Korbes, is a Nobel Prize winner who has written twenty-two novels which describe, with detailed accuracy, twenty-two murders he has committed. The basic device of the parody is that only an author who has really experienced what he writes is deserving of attention. What the jaded reading public demands is a form of vicarious thrill from the uninhibited way of life which Korbes describes: murders *sans phrase*, without motive or rationale, simply as an experience that will serve as raw material for books.

A meek little bookkeeper from a deeply provincial Swiss village devotes his life to detective work in order to establish, beyond a doubt, that Korbes is in fact the unpunished murderer of the twenty-two victims. When he confronts Korbes with what he naïvely believes is a startling revelation, Korbes enlightens him about modern literature in wonderfully cynical language and proceeds to murder him in preparation for a new radio play which he is going to write.

The fictional device which frames the play is that the *Hörspiel* reflects with accuracy the exact course of the action in "real life," that is, that the interview with the bookkeeper takes place simultaneously with the broadcast of the play. The opening of the play is Korbes's long and detailed description of the setting, which is addressed to the audience. The end is a return to the narration of Korbes, now about to write a radio play about the murder of the bookkeeper. The frame is part of the thrust against an extreme form of "realism."

Dürrenmatt's satire on literature manufactured out of personal experiences which are undertaken solely to provide grist for the pen is both witty and cynical. The intent is clearly to amuse, for the bitter, even tragic overtones of *The Meteor*, which touches on the theme in a different manner, are totally lacking here. The naïve literary detective asserts that it is impossible to invent something that doesn't exist somewhere. He admires in Korbes the compactness, precision, coldness, and lack of sentimentality which have established his fame and won him the Nobel Prize. Korbes responds to this praise by complaining that his way of life is very hard on him, that he is driven from murder to murder partly by debts and partly by the necessity of satisfying his public. This complaint is an echo of the fate of Hercules, who rushes from one labor to the next in order to maintain his public image as well as to pay off his creditors.

Korbes, who is without self-pity as much as without pity, says, in a moment of seriousness, that there is no mercy for one who takes up literature as an occupation—a remark that anticipates the attitudes of *The Meteor*. But Korbes insists that he must keep on, since modern literature has to be factual in order to find an audience. He argues that the whole world knows that he has been murdering so that he could write, and has admired him for it. In fact, people write to him to request that they become his next victims.

Dürrenmatt has reversed his usual procedure in writing literary satire, for this play shows literature as something ruthlessly demanding and brutalizing. Usually the reader is presented with literature as mere decoration, as a form of escape from reality, or as a convenient way of avoiding thinking for one's self—this last is especially true of the quotations from the classics which Dürrenmatt adduces. Now he has added the thought that the production of literature requires no more intellectual effort than its consumption. Writing stories turns out to be just as undignified as reading them. But the lesson or "moral" of the play is not its most important aspects. It is a hilarious spoof that should be listened to or read for fun.

In a few years Dürrenmatt progressed from sermons in dialogue form to radio plays of great subtlety and wit. The ease with which the *Hörspiel* lends itself to parable and preaching was at first a temptation, which Dürrenmatt was slow in learning to resist. Dürrenmatt was able to find the style appropriate to a certain subject matter in some radio plays; but in others he succumbed to the freedom which the genre offers. The development of self-discipline and the increasing mastery of medium in Dürrenmatt's career may be observed as clearly in his radio plays as in anything he wrote. A comparison between the awkward technique of simulating a "live" production in *The Double* and the amusing and persuasive method of achieving the same effect in *An Evening in Late Fall* demonstrates his growing control of the skills required by the genre.

CHAPTER 5

The Short Stories

How can an artist survive in an educated world of literates? Perhaps best of all by writing detective stories and putting art in where no one will suspect it. Literature must become so light that it weighs nothing on the scales of today's literary criticism: only in that way will it become weighty again. (*Problems of the Theater*)

D ÜRRENMATT'S short stories may be conveniently divided into two groups. The first consists of detective stories, "The Judge and His Executioner," "The Suspicion," and "The Pledge." The other two stories, "Once a Greek" and "Traps," are less easy to classify. The last-mentioned story needs no further commentary, since the essentials have been given in the discussion of the radio plays. The first two detective stories, both of which originated at the time when Dürrenmatt was still writing the last sketches of "The City," have as their main figure the elderly and ailing commissar of police, Bärlach. Bärlach is a moralist, a man of incorruptible principles, and an amateur philosopher and psychologist to boot. These traits do not necessarily distinguish him from his fictional compeers in many detective stories. What marks him as a typical creation by Dürrenmatt is his manner of philosophizing, his keen sense of the grotesque, and his understanding of moral issues outside of the law and convention. He is a Swiss citizen who has traveled and worked abroad and who has overcome the strictly provincial view. For this reason he should not be mistaken as an ideal, or even representative, citizen of Switzerland. Dürrenmatt does not idealize him, but he ascribes to him a slightly ironic distance from his work and a gentle detachment combined with dedication to moral principles.

The setting of the Bärlach stories is in Dürrenmatt's native section of Switzerland. The author introduces many precise details of local geography and customs, so that the local color constitutes a significant element. In "The Suspicion," the evil doctor—the villain of the story—is called Emmenberger; and this name is probably intended to echo Emmental, the home district of the author. Satire on Swiss foibles is frequent and often amusing. Sometimes it has political implications, as when Dürrenmatt notes that the attitude toward Nazi Germany varies with the times and the general political climate. On a less serious level, Dürrenmatt indulges his penchant for mildly satiric names, although this device is less richly developed than later in "Once a Greek." One of the political parties referred to is called "conservative-liberal-socialist independents." The Swiss police and the military both are gently satirized, especially in "The Judge and His Executioner." Some of the humor is as locally circumscribed as the precise descriptions of landscape and climate; as for example in the remark that a family from Berne has gained from an admixture of Basel blood. As later in "Once a Greek," it seems to rain a great deal in Dürrenmatt's canton; and rain and cold are features of the descriptive background in all the stories. The combination of weather reports and detailed topography lends these works an exact setting; and the sense of precise location invites the reader to visualize the environment in which the action takes place.

The chief interest of the author in these stories lies not so much in the unravelling of a mystery and the suspense connected with it as the revelation of character and motive. The stories are told largely from the point of view of Bärlach, and the development of the plot takes place as a series of successes and insights of the central figure. An ancient and honorable tradition of detective stories is preserved in the fact that Bärlach, old and conservative, is usually at odds with the rest of the police force, which relies on up-to-date methods of crime detection. Their modern techniques are not as effective as the old-fashioned psychology of Bärlach, who is portrayed more as a humanist and keen observer of human nature than as a professional detective relying on modern devices and gadgets. Bärlach is successful in solving the crime because of his understanding of people and their motives. Although he is referred to as a lifelong fighter for justice, his character is sketched in broad strokes rather than fully outlined. Much about him remains at the level of assertion that is not depicted in action.

The style and language in the Bärlach stories are simple, but often rather carelessly handled. In "The Suspicion," the huge Jew

is a fictional phantom and as much a postulate of the imagination
as a convenient agent of rescue. His presence helps to contribute
to an atmosphere of the fairy tale that is inconsistent with the
close attention to detail mentioned above in connection with the
description of the milieu. The ending is a combination of moral
lesson and allegory.

"The Judge and His Executioner" tells the story of how Inspector Bärlach pursues the murderer of a police lieutenant. But for
Bärlach the pursuit of the murderer is more than the routine investigation of a crime, because the case involves an old enemy of
his who is a dedicated criminal-nihilist. For Bärlach the problem
lies in a realm of abstract justice beyond the legal issues: his old
criminal enemy is not even the murderer. Chance, which plays as
large a part in Dürrenmatt's stories as in his plays, enables Bärlach
to set the real murderer against his old enemy in such a way that
they destroy each other. This is a triumph for justice both in the
strictly legal sense and on the level of poetic justice. "The Suspicion" reintroduces Inspector Bärlach, older now and suffering
from an inoperable case of cancer, but willing to spend his last
efforts in bringing to justice a doctor, who, he suspects, is continuing the evil practices of the Nazi concentration camps in a private
sanatorium. Bärlach has himself transferred to this sanatorium, is
recognized by the sadistic doctor Emmenberger, and is saved
from an operation to be performed without anesthesia only after
days of terror and helplessness. A victim of Nazi persecution who
has escaped alive from the torture chambers rescues him at the
last moment.

Although Gulliver, the giant Jew who rescues Bärlach, is not a
credible character, the sanatorium and Emmenberger, who tor-
tures his victims, are impressive symbols of the society which
emerged from the Second World War. Emmenberger is able to
lure patients into his hospital and torture them because they offer
no resistance, even submit willingly to his superior but perverted
will power. Man's willingness to submit to evil without resisting it,
and the fear and confusion that arise in those who suffer, are portrayed in the story of the sanatorium. The meek acceptance by the
patients of the sadistic cure—always fatal—that Emmenberger
offers symbolizes the readiness of desperate or frustrated people
to turn for relief to anyone who offers a panacea. The introduction
of a dwarf and a giant into this atmosphere emphasizes the au-

thor's allegorical intent. The suggestion is that the sanatorium is a model of our world, where perversion is aided by its victims and where only a supreme act of will can create freedom. But to read such philosophical implications into the work is perhaps to take too seriously a story written primarily as entertainment.[1] In "The Judge and His Executioner," Dürrenmatt himself warns against "the vanity of a writer who wants to be taken seriously."

I *"The Pledge"*

Nothing is more horrible than a genius who stumbles because of something idiotic.

"The Pledge" has the ironic subtitle "A Requiem for the Detective Story." This parodistic farewell to the genre grew out of a film scenario written as a warning against sex crimes committed against minors. The plot of the short story carries over from the film version the murder of a child by an insane pervert, but the emphasis has shifted from the criminal to the fate of the detective who seeks to solve the mystery of the crime. It is one of the few works by Dürrenmatt which use a frame as an essential device in the telling of the story. This narrative frame is related by the author in the first person, and the central plot is told in the first person by the former police inspector of the canton Zurich.

The opening of the story parodies the classics (this time *Faust,* Part II) in the accustomed manner. The author, a not-too-successful writer of detective stories, complains that people nowadays prefer to go to lectures on the problems of writing detective mysteries. This remark prompts a listener—the former inspector (who says he prefers Max Frisch to the author)—to remind the author on the many faults and weaknesses of the modern detective story. He notes that they usually end with the punishment of the criminal, not as structural necessity, but rather for moral reasons and as a kind of deception and propaganda demanded by public morals. In addition, he points out that the plot structure is always logical, as in a chess game, and therefore subject to logical analysis and solution. No real role is assigned to pure chance, or accident. By this he does not mean fate, destiny, or the working out of a grand cosmic design, but just ordinary chance. To illustrate his point, he reminisces about a case which occurred nine years ago.

As the story of the inspector unfolds, it immediately becomes clear that it is the tale of a fixed idea. The inspector introduces his narrative by viewing the sad results of the fixation: he takes the author to visit a former police detective who is far gone in drunkenness and degeneracy, and this as the result of having made a promise (whence the title of the story) to find the murderer of a young girl. Matthäi, as the former detective is called, is a fanatic of justice, and as such he is akin to Mr. Mississippi and others whom the reader has come to know in Dürrenmatt's works. He is a humorless and rigidly consistent monomaniac, and the crowning irony of the story—revealed only at the end—is that all the time he was right in his obsession. But he was ruined by an accident, for the murderer, whom otherwise Matthäi would surely have caught, was killed in an auto accident before the trap set by Matthäi could be sprung. The detective, not knowing of this accidental death, waited and pursued his plan for capture for years, until he became totally absorbed by his obsession and ruined by stupor and liquor. He became the victim of his own brilliant logical reasoning and was undone by the humorless persistence with which he clung to his conclusions.

Like many other champions of justice, Matthäi is completely lacking in humanity and common sense. He maintains his faith in his logical reasoning to the point of absurdity, resisting the cumulative empirical evidence that time provides. The ruin of a brilliant mind becomes the dominant theme of the story, which is among the cruelest that Dürrenmatt has ever written. Even minor scenes, such as that in which the inspector takes leave of the dying widow of the murderer, are marked by a grim humor. The inspector uses the customary formula of farewell, "leb wohl," as he leaves her dying. The use of fairy-tale motifs and elements in the story is more terrible and gruesome than grotesque, for cruelty and pain rather than the redeeming qualities of the grotesque, which at its best offers release and relief through its own incongruous nature, and is therefore always potentially humorous, are presented. The mixture of grimness and wit in a remark like Frau Ill's "a friendly fate" is characteristic for Dürrenmatt's use of the grotesque at its best. Where gruesomeness is predominant, as in this story, the mood effected is quite different from that produced by a delicate balance of the macabre and the incongruous.

The story is more than merely a requiem for the detective story, for it is also one of Dürrenmatt's parables of justice. Much more strikingly and effectively than in the earlier stories, which are also, in their own way, concerned with justice, Dürrenmatt has portrayed with brutal irony the difficulties of securing justice in a world where chance and accident may make a mockery of man's intelligence. Since the divine ordering of things seems to prevent cosmic justice, or at least obscure it from men's eyes, the individual's personal responsibility in seeking the right and just path becomes all the greater. This was the message of the Bärlach stories, in which personal integrity triumphed in spite of chance. But "The Pledge" illustrates the crucial role of chance in men's lives and demonstrates man's inability to understand the world by means of his reason. However, it should be noted that the style of the story is not nearly as abstract as our discussion of it. The language is casual and conversational and by no means sententious.

Some of the scenes are described by the inspector as being "painful and grotesque." As is customary in Dürrenmatt's stories, there are long passages describing rainy weather. The narrator, a philosopher with a sense of humor, is sensitive to weather and landscape, but above all he has a fine feeling for human weakness and for the imperfection of this world. But this has not made him a cynic; on the contrary, he concludes his narrative by pointing out to the author that the most important thing in life is how one accepts the absurd and the incommensurable. His final message is that our reason hardly illumines the world we live in, and this fact we must learn to accept.

II   *"Once a Greek"*

The president: The miracle that happened to you two is only possible through love and without love will turn into a farce.

The subtitle of this story reads "A Prose Comedy," but it might well have been "A Modern Fairy Tale," for the atmosphere of a fairy tale is sustained throughout this brightest and most lighthearted of Dürrenmatt's narratives. The story opens with the statement that it has been raining for weeks. Cold and rain play an important role, especially in the early part of the book. It is raining when Archilochos first meets his fairy-land lady Chloe, but the weather clears up when they take their first walk together. Cold is only partly meteorological, since coldness on the part of people also matters. The thaw in the weather is matched by a general thaw in people's attitudes and behavior, for the weather and the responses of human beings are kept in harmony throughout. The joy in details and the precise and suggestive descriptions of the environment start in the first paragraph. But as the author proceeds, the reader soon becomes aware that a "reality" is being presented that is made up of baroque details, and that the sum of the observations has come to portray a kind of fairy land filled with mild grotesqueries and containing a quite surrealistic atmosphere. The technique of using apparently concrete observations and details to build up a total image that is fantastic reminds one both of Kafka's novels and Dürrenmatt's own early prose. The story was written during composition of *The Visit*, but it lacks the tragic tone of the play and conveys a spirit of fun and fantasy quite removed from it.

The Swiss citizen Arnolph Archilochos, whose ancestors came from Greece to Switzerland, is a humble bookkeeper in the giant concern of Petit-Paysan. He is a vegetarian and teetotaler with a strict set of rules for the conduct of life. He is a devoted member of the Old-new Presbyterians of the Next-to-last Christians. He is also the proud possessor of a firm moral world order. At the head of the representatives of this world order, as his moral and spiritual guides, stand the president of the state, while the second place is held by the bishop, the third by Mr. Petit-Paysan, and fourth place is occupied by the modernistic painter, Passap. Archilochos is quite serious in his reverence for these models of virtue and exemplary living, for he is a humorless fanatic of virtue, which makes him a relative of many other figures in Dürrenmatt's works. But Dürrenmatt is smiling here, and the poor Greek, with his hopelessly heterogeneous models of virtue, is not caricatured in the grim way in which Matthäi was. Arnolph's brother Bibi is a happy good-for-nothing who sponges shamelessly on Arnolph; yet he is number eight in the moral world order. This odd assembly of moral heroes is meant both to be amusing and to illustrate the confusion that exists in Arnolph's unawakened mind.

At the mature and settled age of forty-five, Arnolph decides to marry. In order to find a wife he places an advertisement in a newspaper: Greek man seeks Greek girl. The answer to this notice is a gorgeous young vision of loveliness, a Greek lady named Chloe. She is so beautiful and attractive that Arnolph can hardly believe it. She seems to come from fairy lands beyond the real world. And now the trial by miracle begins, for Arnolph is promoted to director of the great Petit-Paysan concern, the bishop receives him and promises to perform the wedding ceremony, people greet him on the street, he is suddenly wealthy, famous, and a member of the world church council, and miracles of undeserved success in all fields descend upon him. At first he bears the burden of his success with the heroic fortitude of a Job withstanding the outrages of misfortune. But at the wedding he suddenly realizes the reason for all the strange things that have happened: Chloe is a courtesan with city-wide connections. Her former clients—Arnolph's models of virtue—are the sponsors of the sudden turn of fortune. Arnolph races out of the church in shame, rage, and despair, and is recruited by the Communist Fahrcks for an assassination attempt on the president's life. But the president (a former friend of Chloe), whom Arnolph reaches at night by scaling the façade of the building, receives him kindly and lectures him on love. He points out that Chloe is, if viewed properly, a genius of love, that the whole affair is a miracle, an act of grace which came to Arnolph beyond his just deserts.

During the nocturnal interview with the president, Arnolph experiences an awaking and a renewal of his whole being. As he eats meat, smokes, and drinks wine, both the words and the manner of the president help him to achieve the balance and calm perspective of maturity for the first time in his life. He completes a dialectical process, moving from moral fanaticism as a "pure fool" through absurdity and profound despair to an awakening to his true self. Tranquillity and peace come to his soul, and an "incomprehensible serenity" possesses him as he listens to the words of the president.

Armed with his new insights, Arnolph returns to his home to throw out the bums and whores who have gathered there with his brother Bibi. In his fury, he cleans house with astonishing vigor, raping, wrecking, beating up, and tossing out the scoundrels. The first conclusion of the story leaves him standing outside the house, having lost his glasses (but having regained his sight), covered with blood and dirt, and still in his wedding suit.

As in so many of Dürrenmatt's works, the climax of the story is the achievement of an insight and a revelation of reality. And typical, too, is the fact that it is evidenced in a scene of grandiose

violence and wild action. Arnolph has returned to reality and has
attained a comprehension of the world as it really is, which his
former moral world order had prevented. This newly acquired
understanding of himself is the substance of the first ending.
Compared to "Traps," where the insight achieved by the hero led
to his suicide, it is a happy ending. But Dürrenmatt wished to
continue his comedy in a more obvious way too. A second ending,
for lending libraries, is therefore added—one with a happy outcome, an ironic triumph of love that reunites Arnolph and Chloe
in Greece, the land of their longing. The first ending shows the
failure of a moral fanatic to pass the test of a miracle of love; the
second is written for sentimental old maids and aunts who wish to
have a gentle moral added to a happy ending. Dürrenmatt rarely
signals so openly the fact that he is writing with tongue in cheek
as in the appended ending.

As Madame Bieler rightly remarks, the name Arnolph Archilochos is impossible. Archilochos was also the name of an ancient
Greek lyric poet and writer of lampoons. Horace speaks of the
"rage" of Archilochos, and Hadrian calls his verses "raging iam-
bics." Arnolph is compared to the Greek war god Ares by the
painter Passap (whose name is a deliberate palindrome—his pictures may be seen backwards as well as forwards) who recognizes
the potential in him which is not realized until the grotesque
scene of battle when he expels Bibi and his gang. Fahrcks is, of
course, an echo of Marx. Passap lives in the suggestively named
Rue Funèbre. Petit-Paysan, or little peasant, is said to be modeled
on a real person in Zurich. But in addition to the names, whose
comic effect is rather obvious, Dürrenmatt has also made clever
use of several clichés. The phrases "pure fool" and "city-wide
prostitute" are the starting points of a story whose fairy-tale atmosphere is counterpointed with more mundane details such as
the noisy plumbing in Arnolph's rented room. The unctuous words
of the bishop, a lover of Chloe's, clash with his conduct. The president, always presented in government propaganda as a teetotaler
who prefers milk, turns out to be a lover of good liquor. Throughout the story, slogans and propaganda are in contrast with reality,
a reality of the kind which Arnolph only gradually learns to see.

The visual imagery used to show both Arnolph's initial blindness and to indicate his growing awareness of reality cannot be
properly accounted for without retelling most of the story. Dür-

renmatt employs several leitmotifs, one of the best being Arnolph's eyesight. He is shortsighted and believes no evil, not
even of Bibi. He only learns to see after his glasses have been
broken in the monumental battle. Yet he does have a kind of in-
tuition, for Passap's pictures—weirdly geometric and fiercely non-
representational—yield their secrets immediately to Arnolph, who
recognizes the nude Chloe in a maze of lines, ellipses, and parabo-
las. At the same time, he tolerates and contributes to the support
of his brother Bibi, who has a wife, two mistresses, and seven
children as well as numerous dubious hangers-on.

Much of the charm of the story lies in the style and clever use of
language to obtain a wide range of effects. Sometimes the language is sententious and pompous, very often it is extravagant,
and it is always full of satiric thrusts. The amount of detail ex-
pended on satirizing the vastly complex bureaucracy of Petit-
Paysan is excessive and a little tiring. The briefer thrusts are more
amusing. Literary satire on the purely ornamental use of the classics is something the reader has come to expect, and this story is
not disappointing in this regard. This time Petit-Paysan is carrying
a thin-paper edition of Hölderlin when he receives Archilochos.
Shortly thereafter he quotes the Earth-Spirit of Goethe's *Faust*.
Hyperbole in visual imagery is a favorite technique of Dürrenmatt's and is responsible for numerous comic effects in this story.
The phrase "frozen stiff" is usually to be understood figuratively,
but Dürrenmatt describes Nadelöhr as being very literally frozen
into immobility and clattering like a Glockenspiel. Prostitutes are
described as standing about in flocks like black birds. At the wedding, street urchins hang on the street lights like grapes dirtied by
chalk. Such hyperbole is usually so controlled that it appears in
the midst of more realistic description as a kind of condiment,
spicing the probable with the wildly improbable. More than most
of Dürrenmatt's prose this story may be reread with the pleasure
of discovering new motifs and minor excellencies of composition
and of realizing the suggestive and premonitional force of the
countless *double-entendres*.[2]

Dürrenmatt's short stories are not responsible for his fame, although they have contributed greatly to his popularity with the
reading public. Stories like "Traps" and "Once a Greek" are successful literary works in their own right and not merely chips from
the workbench of a great playwright. Like the plays, they are all

thematically concerned with the problem of justice in an imperfect world, and therefore they help to round out the portrait of a major dramatist of our time. In style and language they are constructed of the same elements that form the plays, but with less closely knit dialogue, a greater sense of freedom and play for its own sake, and the more obvious purpose of sheer entertainment. The use of grotesqueness is similar to that found in the larger works, but without the will to achieve universality or breadth of implication and validity. The characters and the plots are more personal, intimate, and concerned with private, individual fates rather than with the larger cosmic issues of the plays. All the qualities of Dürrenmatt's works for the stage are present in profusion, but on a smaller, more modest scale. Sometimes the concentration in a smaller genre allows effects as striking as those of the plays, but more often the stories are written in a more subdued key and aim at smaller targets than those which Dürrenmatt usually projects on the stage. For the student of Dürrenmatt they are rewarding reading both for pleasure and for a broader understanding of the author's art.

CHAPTER 6

The Critical Writings and Summary

Misunderstandings creep in, because people desperately search
the henyard of my dramas for the egg of explanation which
I steadfastly refuse to lay. (*Problems of the Theater*)

FOR many years Dürrenmatt was known as a theorist of drama
only through the small volume *Problems of the Theater*, published in 1955. The book attracted immediate attention, and it has
been quoted and referred to frequently ever since its appearance.[1] *Problems of the Theater* was originally the manuscript of a
lecture which Dürrenmatt gave in the fall of 1954 and the spring
of 1955 in various cities of Switzerland and West Germany. Many
of the other items now contained in *Writings and Speeches on the
Theater*[2] were also originally lectures or speeches and have retained their character of dialogue with an audience. There are, to
be sure, reviews which were published in journals, and the annotations appended to several of the plays are reprinted in the volume.
But the dominant tone of the book is that of living speech, and the
dialogue situation is simulated even in those essays which were
not originally lectures. The voice of the speaker addressing an audience which is invited to participate and follow can be heard
even in those items which are most obviously essays written as
private philosophical musings. The stance of the lecturer is clearly
Dürrenmatt's favorite position, since it allows him to speak infor-
mally, with digressions, with appeals to a public, and always with
irony and distance. Only rarely does he drop his mask and speak
in a straightforward confessional form. His essays, therefore, are
to be read with as much alertness for irony and humor as his plays
or stories. His personal commitment to the ideas expressed is always evident, but even when commenting on his own works he is
able to maintain his modesty and objectivity.

All the essays are marked by Dürrenmatt's highly individual
style and personality, but in spite of the wealth of insights con-

tained in the volume no unified, coherent system of dramaturgy is presented. Dürrenmatt is quite frank about his attitudes and views on specific subjects, but he has never formulated a concise theory of drama or attempted to develop a comprehensive philosophy of the theater. His views have changed over the years, as he gladly admits, and consistency is not a virtue which he values highly. Miss Brock-Sulzer has chosen as a motto for her volume the Dürrenmatt aphorism: "He who never contradicts himself will never be read again." This explains why some short stories have been reworked as radio plays, and *Hercules*, originally a radio play, has been recast as a stage play, while *Frank V* has been redone for television. Some plays, notably *Romulus* and *Frank V*, have been published in several versions.

Dürrenmatt tends to view his texts as working models, capable of refashioning and susceptible to recasting at any time. Rehearsals for a *première* always led to revisions and corrections, and after the first productions the manuscripts were usually recast for publication.[3] "To rework a play is the attempt to educate it. It is a problematical task, but it belongs to the necessities of our profession." [4] Dürrenmatt's profession is writing, which he considers a business like any other.[5] Every plot or subject matter, he believes, has a life of its own and seeks a form of expression which is adequate to it. The proof that the solution has been found and that the content has attained its proper form is, in the case of plays, only to be demonstrated on the stage: "The stage is always the author's teacher, and he can always learn from it." [6]

For two years, from 1951 to 1953, Dürrenmatt wrote theater reviews for the *Weltwoche* of Zurich. Much earlier than that he had attempted to formulate his own views on art and the theater, and indeed critical assessments of the nature of the theater accompany his entire creative career. Since the publication of *Problems of the Theater*, Dürrenmatt's tendency to comment critically on his own works and to write guidelines for their understanding has increased with every passing year.[7] Nevertheless he has always had reservations about theorizing, has usually appeared somewhat embarrassed, and has steadfastly refused to speak in solemn tones about the meaning of literature.

In spite of his activity as theater critic, disparaging remarks about critics and theater criticism in general may be found in every volume of Dürrenmatt's writing. His antagonism to critics is

one of the consistent themes in all his works.[8] He has often felt
that his plays were not understood on the basis of the dramatic
presentation, but were judged by abstract or a priori standards
which were not relevant to the reality of the drama. In the course
of his running battle with the critics, his own tone has become
sharper and more insistently didactic. In lectures and essays he
has preserved both his good humor and his self-directed irony, but
in the polemics with critics and in his annotations a note of irritation has crept in. When one compares the good-humored annotations appended to the earlier plays, such as *Romulus,* with the
almost strident tone of the "twenty points" in defense of *The Meteor* (especially the first three points and the nineteenth), the
change in Dürrenmatt's attitude toward the public and the critics
becomes immediately apparent. He is no longer content merely to
make suggestions for the staging of his dramas; for he now considers it necessary to prescribe the rules according to which criticism should proceed.

All those critical writings, essays, and speeches which Dürrenmatt wished to have published, have now been collected in one
volume by Miss Brock-Sulzer. The volume contains sixty-six
items: addresses and lectures, theoretical discourses and autobiographical reports, reviews, aphorisms, and the appended notes
and "points" to his plays. The dates of composition range from
1947 to 1965. In her introduction Miss Brock-Sulzer emphasizes
that several of these pieces were written in self-defense. But the
aggressive tone of many of them belies this assertion, and the posture of attack is more congenial to Dürrenmatt than that of defense. The book now gathers together pieces published in different places, and it includes items never before published. Many of
the essays are occasional pieces, prompted by a performance or a
particular work which came to Dürrenmatt's attention. Others are
longer theoretical statements of important autobiographical content. The central essays are *Problems of the Theater* and the
speech in acceptance of the Schiller Prize in Mannheim in 1959.
The book is an extended confession of devotion to drama and the
theater. But just because of this personal tone and the fact that
many of the essays are written in response to a mood or a particular moment, the reader will enjoy the book most by reading the
individual items as independent units.

Dürrenmatt is under no illusions concerning the effectiveness of presenting theories of the drama to the public. He is quite conscious of the fact that a dramaturgical theory is always specific to the works of a particular author, or even more drastically, to one special work. He presents his theory, therefore, as a practitioner and constantly emphasizes the fact that his thoughts about his work arise during and after the completion of a play and not as abstract postulates which predetermine the work. He recommends caution with regard to a dramatist's theorizing, and the reader will do well to remember this when reading Dürrenmatt —he asserts that a dramatist must yield to his inspiration (*"Einfälle"*) and that only what he is working on at the moment seems really important. By applying his own warning to his statements, one can then take with a grain of salt such assertions as the famous statement that only comedy speaks to our condition. Although Dürrenmatt makes a persuasive case for this claim, the reader must keep in mind that the statement is made *ad hoc* and as commentary on Dürrenmatt's own recent work. It is just as convincing to take the opposite position, namely that tragedy is more cheerful and optimistic than comedy, and that in our time and condition it represents a celebration of human freedom and the triumph over despair. Modish pessimism about the state of the world is perhaps the task of comedy, which deals with man's aberrations and folly, whereas tragedy deals with man's potential nobility even in the destruction of this nobility.[9]

When he speaks as a theoretician, Dürrenmatt's stance is usually ambivalent. On the one hand he emphasizes the practical nature of his undertaking; on the other he feels the necessity of explication and of a theoretical accounting for his work. The conflicting urges are the source of tensions which can be observed in most of his writing on the theater. The urge to explain and the contrary feeling that explanation is no substitute for practical work are strikingly evident in interview situations. Dürrenmatt can be very sly and scurrilous in an interview. His answers to questions are often evasive and deliberately calculated to lead the interviewer onto other paths of discussion. His efforts to divert his questioner from the subject at hand may take the form of references to his love of painting, his hobbies, or his fondness for certain other dramatists. The deftness and skill displayed in such situations is often amusing, but it can also be misleading by the avoidance of direct answers.[10] Dürrenmatt shuns big words and grandiose phrases, both because he finds them suspect and devoid of real meaning and because he wishes to avoid too convenient labels. Understatement, ironic allusions, and evasive paraphrases of his intent are his preferred forms of guardedly stating his true opinions. A sense of distance and the desire for privacy protect him at all times and prevent naïve revelations of himself. His remark that the film is indecent in its overexposure and destruction of privacy is typical of his attitude.

The public and the critics have gradually learned to respect Dürrenmatt's desire for privacy and have become accustomed to his reserved manner. In spite of his success and fame, Dürrenmatt has rejected any temptation to appear as a spokesman or champion of his native country, although he has always been conscious of his origins, and in his own way, true to them. When he does speak autobiographically, he likes to emphasize his birth and childhood in provincial Switzerland. Switzerland is the starting point of all his thoughts and the constant reference point for his orientation. To be Swiss in today's world of big powers is a special challenge, and to be a Swiss author is even more complex and difficult. Dürrenmatt is well aware of the problems and difficulties, and he has slipped into his works many sly references to the country and its national traits. Mild irony and gentle witticisms are the forms of reference to Swiss foibles in general, but the tone of his allusions is sharper when he is speaking of Swiss writers. At times one hears faint autobiographical echoes, with the humor and irony which always accompany them. In *The Suspicion* he says that it is difficult enough for a poet to have to live in Switzerland, but it is ten times harder to have to make a living there.

Dürrenmatt's preference for hiding behind an analogy and of revealing his true feelings indirectly is nicely illustrated by the lecture which he gave in New York.[11] Stimulated by the atmosphere of the city in a country that is one of the superpowers and one toward which his attitude may be described as reserved ambivalence, he chose to take the fictional case of a dramatist from the tiny state of Liechtenstein. Rather than discuss the problems that arise in the modern world for a dramatist from Switzerland, he used the state of Liechtenstein as a cover under the protection of which he could make his instructive autobiographical remarks:

I can imagine . . . a writer, who is a Liechtensteiner and takes great pleasure in being one, and for whom Liechtenstein is much more than the 61 square miles which it actually measures. For this writer Liechtenstein will become a model of the world. He will intensify it by broadening it, and will make a Babylon out of Vaduz and a Nebukadnezar out of its ruling prince. The Liechtensteiners will protest . . . but this writer will not only be played in St. Gall, he will become international because the world will be mirrored in his invented Liechtenstein. This writer from Liechtenstein will have to keep employing new ideas and making ever new models of the world out of Liechtenstein, and he will have to strike out on new paths as a dramatist. These new paths will be the right ones, simply because for him there are no others.

The validity of these remarks for Dürrenmatt's own condition is so obvious as to need no commentary. The lecture continues with the praise of a small state that accepts its role in the world, since such a state offers a writer great freedom. Most especially it offers the writer the freedom "to accept government as what it should be, namely as a technical necessity and not as a man-eating myth." The lecture closes on the note that creative writing has its essential basis in freedom, and that it is in fact one of the few positive proofs of the existence of freedom. The lecture thus characteristically moves from the veiled and indirectly autobiographical to statements of general validity and of an impersonal nature. Dürrenmatt has always been more interested in presenting his views than his personality.

Few authors are the best commentators on their own works, and Dürrenmatt is no exception to this general rule. Most critics would agree that he is not the best explicator of his own works; yet one must take seriously the comments which he has made, since they indicate the development in his thinking and highlight his constant concerns. Certain themes recur in varying form within his essays, sometimes emphatically as central thoughts, sometimes only as passing comments. For example, his ambivalent attitude toward both Schiller and Brecht, compounded of respect and distance, finds various forms of expression and reveals shifting emphases, whereas his unvarying admiration of Nestroy and Aristophanes is expressed in several essays and interviews. It is instructive to note Dürrenmatt's various attitudes toward the visual aspects of a play, if we may choose just one facet of his

dramaturgy. Literal duplication of natural environments may
have the effect of working directly against the suggestive quality
of a play, thereby distracting the audience from the enchantment
evoked by the dialogue. As Dürrenmatt discovered quite early in
his career, there are limits to the creation of a total optical illusion
on the stage. The clutter of visual detail can impede, if not actually prevent, the suspension of disbelief, thus becoming an unintentional form of estrangement: "The stage scenery is not decoration, rather it is a part of the interpretation. . . ." [12]

Dürrenmatt's concern with the problems of stage scenery, optical effects, and general visual quality has remained constant, but
in both theory and practice he has moved from the impossibly
extravagant effects of *It Is Written* to the sparse *décor* of *The
Physicists*. The early plays make extraordinary demands on the
use of stage properties, often without supplying sufficient dramatic material in either action or dialogue to sustain it. Where too
much visual representation is required, as in the luxuriant stage
directions for *It Is Written*, the scenery attains its own lush
growth independently of the action, or, what is worse, becomes a
substitute for action, as in the final tableau of this play. Dürrenmatt's belated realization of this leads to scenic effects which are
more closely integrated with the dialogue, as in *Romulus* or the
Marriage of Mr. Mississippi. After clarifying his theoretical position, as much for himself as for his public, in *Problems of the
Theater*, his stage directions, even when lavish, tend to become
functional reinforcements of the dialogue. The long and detailed
stage directions for *The Physicists* seem to be a reversion to earlier
practice, but are clearly intended for the reader and have little
application to the scene which the audience actually sees. At the
very beginning of his career, Dürrenmatt was well aware that the
stage can falsify a play, but it took years until this theoretical
insight was consistently put into practice. [13]

Since *Problems of the Theater* is now easily available in translation, there is a danger that this document, so frequently cited in
the critical literature, will come to represent to English-speaking
people the sum of Dürrenmatt's theoretical wisdom. The book,
which represents the author's thoughts at a certain stage in his
development, now seems dated in style and attitude and super-
seded by his subsequent practice. Thus, for example, he dismisses
as mere prejudice the requirement that a major character in a play

must develop, although the focal point of interest in *The Visit* is the transformation which Ill undergoes. He indulges in extended polemics with the Aristotelian unities of time, place, and action, apparently refuting their validity and laying them to rest; but the striking thing about the formal structure of both *The Physicists* and *The Meteor* is this strict adherence to the unities. The book contains many rather obvious statements about drama, assertions that are stated with great assurance but without supporting evidence, discussion of dead or otiose issues; and all in all it serves more to reveal Dürrenmatt's feelings about the theater than to provide a systematic dramaturgy. In spite of the shortcomings just enumerated, it remains one of the more interesting and important documents by a practicing dramatist of our times.

The book opens with two basic assertions: that the author is not the purveyor of an ideology and that his dramatic theory is primarily that of a practical worker in the theater. The first negative statement receives great emphasis, yet it is one that demands closer examination. Dürrenmatt himself states that the view of the world which a dramatist has will influence his dramaturgy and determine his themes. While denying adherence to any abstract philosophy, he also maintains that the drama is inevitably an attempt to represent on the stage the world as the author sees it. He compares the drama to a mirror which reflects the world,[14] but behind this comparison stands a very personal, private view of the world. It is a question of how "the world of today appears to us." Dürrenmatt writes:

Schiller wrote the way he did because the world in which he lived could still be mirrored in the world which he described and which he created as a historian. Just barely. Napoleon, after all, was the last hero in the old sense of the word. The world of today, as it appears to us, can hardly be mastered through the form of Schiller's historical drama, because we no longer find tragic heroes, but only tragedies staged by world butchers and carried out by meat-grinding machines. One can no longer make Wallensteins out of Hitler and Stalin. Their power is so gigantic that they themselves are only fortuitous and external forms of this power, and can be replaced at will, and the disaster associated especially with the first and, to a degree, with the second has become too widely ramified, too confused, too cruel and too mechanical and often also simply too meaningless. Wallenstein's power is still apparent, whereas power today is only minimally visible, since like an iceberg the largest part is sunk in faceless abstraction. Schiller's drama presupposes a visible world. . . . Today's state has, however, become impossible to survey, anonymous and bureaucratic. . . . Genuinely representative people are lacking and the tragic heroes have no name. Today's world can be better represented by a small profiteer, by a secretary or a policeman than by a congressman or a chancellor of state. Art only reaches the victim, if it reaches human beings at all, and does not penetrate to those with power. Creon's secretaries take care of the case of Antigone.[15]

This oft-quoted passage is typical in both its content and form, since Dürrenmatt here, as so often, presents his personal view of the world and then proceeds to draw the logical conclusions from his private premises. As a form of argument the line of reasoning adopted here is as characteristic of his essay as the deductions which he makes. Tragedy presupposes an ordered, "visible" world in which there is private responsibility. Since in the modern world there are no individuals who are responsible, no one in particular is guilty. "Everything is dragged along and everyone gets caught somewhere in the course of events. We are all collectively guilty . . . guilt can only exist as a personal achievement, as a religious deed. Comedy alone gets at our problems." [16] We are again dealing with a famous quotation, and again the line of reasoning seems, at first sight, to be logically compelling. There is, however, a logical leap from the assertion that tragedy is impossible to the statement that comedy alone is suitable for our times. Dürrenmatt's expository prose is persuasive, however, even where it is not logical, and it has the ring of conviction even where it is inconsistent.[17] In practice Dürrenmatt's analysis of the world situation and the conclusions which the dramatist must draw from it are neither binding nor normative for the structure of his dramas. But it is important to know his basic stance, for he has been remarkably consistent, even tenacious, in his view of the world. And every work he has ever published reflects his *Weltanschauung*. His first play has as its theme man's search for God presented in grotesque, shocking terms; his latest play, *The Meteor,* has the rejection of the search for God as its theme, presented in a scurrilous manner.

In matters of principle Dürrenmatt has always been firm and unyielding. His rejection of abstract rules and of all approaches to drama which are not primarily practical can be found throughout his career. "For me the stage does not represent a field for theories, ideologies and statements, but an instrument whose possibilities I seek to discover by playing along with it." [18] His modest assessment of the importance of art is expressed in a well-known quotation: "Nothing is more dangerous for the artist than the overestimation of art. Art can stand any kind of underestimation. In the solemn incense smoke of today's absolute art it can suffocate." [19] His attitude toward style and language is as consistent as his famous dictum that comedy is the only form of drama adequate to our situation.[20] His contention that modern drama, as it reflects the modern world, cannot present a hero in the traditional sense has been as stubbornly maintained as his belief that a writer must have the courage to follow his inspiration (*"Einfälle"*).[21]

Such constancy would not be possible without a firm and unchanging view of the world combined with the conviction that drama must reflect the world of today. Every great writer has recreated the contemporary world around him, Dürrenmatt maintains, and must therefore possess a world view which provides a perspective. In a lecture given in 1956,[22] while rejecting the role of the philosophical thinker and while maintaining that he had great difficulty and felt some embarrassment in speaking about the meaning of poetry, he admitted that he wrote because he felt the urge to write and because he loved to tell stories without, however, feeling the compulsion to solve the riddles of the world while telling them. After this personal remark which, like so many of his statements about himself, is provocative both for what it admits and for what it conceals, he went on to explain that the world and our modern thinking about it have become so abstract and mathematical that they elude representation in language. Modern man, he believes, sees himself increasingly surrounded by things which he uses and manipulates but does not understand, and whose essential nature he cannot visualize. What is visible in our world is technology and its apparatus. "Today man lives in a world which he knows less than we assume. He has lost his image and has become a victim of images." [23] The abstract formulas of the scientists make the layman only more nervous and create the feeling that he is living in a world that is incomprehensible and hostile. This feeling of insecurity makes him an easy victim of simplifying propaganda and soothing slogans. It is Dürrenmatt's sincerest wish not to add to the easy formulas or simplistic explanations. The more baffling the world seems to become, the more urgent it is not to accept the facile solutions of ideology.

The concern for man's social relationships and for the problems of community living, so evident in his plays, forms an essential part of his theoretical writings. The deep moral and ethical basis of all of Dürrenmatt's work, derived from his own, personal understanding of Christian precepts, leads to the challenging search for humanity and decency in all his writings.[24] He sees the individual as estranged from the world, not only on a cosmic level where failure to understand international politics or the atom bomb might lead to despair, but in the basic societal relationships such as family, village community, and other interpersonal situations. In the plays, the failure of a marriage is frequently chosen as the analogue to the disintegration of a larger social ordering. In one of his essays he writes:

The part no longer is contained in the whole, the individual no longer in the total order, nor man in humanity. There remains for the individual only the feeling of impotence and of having been passed over, of not being able to interfere or to determine his fate, and of having to take cover in order not to be ruined. But also there is the presentiment of a great liberation, of new possibilities, and the feeling that the time has come to perform one's tasks with decision and courage.[25]

The quotation above is characteristic in its mixture of hope and despair. In the confused world of today Dürrenmatt turns to art as an adventure, a risk, a form of conquest, and a demonstration of freedom and courage. He became a writer, he claims, in order to irritate people; he wants to be "uncomfortable and protest and warn as a gadfly on the horse of state." [26] But he does not expect that his warning will save the world, nor does he wish to produce only didactic dramas with warnings, protests, and moralizing messages: "Everything moral and didactic must happen unintentionally in the drama. I can give an answer to a question only to him who himself has the courage: that is the cruel, human limitation of art. By itself art is impotent, and it is not a consolation or a religion, but only a sign that in the midst of the general despair somewhere there is someone who does not despair. I can do no more than give this sign. The writer can only fulfill his moral task —I would like to use this word—if he is an anarchist." [27] The writer is, therefore, not primarily and directly a moralist, even when he presents something from which a moral may be derived. The view that the theater should not be first and foremost an educational institution does not mean that the public may not learn and draw inferences from the stage. Dürrenmatt has great faith in the audience and its power to understand. It is in fact his trust in the imagination of the public and its untutored sense of where the meaning lies that renders the indirect and inferential morality of Dürrenmatt's plays possible.[28] Dürrenmatt has always assigned an important role to the public, which has responded by acclaiming most of his plays.

The theory of the impotence of the individual—his inability to change or improve the world or halt the march of history—is a basic tenet of Dürrenmatt's that we have seen illustrated in the tragicomic fate of Romulus, the absurd failure of Mr. Mississippi's reforms, and the resignation in defeat of the physicist Möbius, to mention only some of the most striking examples. These tragicomic failures represent only the negative aspect of the theory, however; for Dürrenmatt, who is always torn between hope and despair, has also drawn quite positive conclusions from this same premise: man can still redeem himself, preserve or recapture his personal integrity, and save his own soul. The possibility of private salvation is the complement to the inability to redeem others or achieve political solutions in a community. "The world as a whole is in confusion, too much must be paid for now, and humanity has increased in numbers too quickly. The world of the individual, on the other hand, can still be mastered, and here guilt and atonement can still be found. Only in the private sphere can today's world still be in order and peace be achieved." [29]

In the public sphere there exist disorder and conflict, and this is the state of the world depicted in Dürrenmatt's writings. He thinks of art as an adventure and playwriting as a form of combat. He conceives of our atomic age as trembling on the brink of a total disaster. Our world is full of monstrous possibilities which may be realized at any moment. This apocalyptic view of the world stands behind all of his thinking and permeates it to such an extent that the breakthrough of the monstrous and horrible is possible at any time in any of his plays and stories. The monstrous in human life is reflected in the outrageous and grotesque elements in his plays, which are the visible signs of a moral abyss hidden under the surface of our civilization. Dürrenmatt's theoretical mastery of the principles involved may be observed in such essays as *Problems of the Theater* or "Notes on Comedy." In practice his application of techniques admirably explicated in theory may vary greatly: *The Visit* demonstrates the demonic and cruel power of economic forces by the whole thrust of the action and is a powerful play just for this reason, whereas *Frank V*, which takes economic forces directly as its theme, is unsuccessful and weak precisely because of the direct approach in which the unmasking has taken place before the play begins. The clarity and profundity of Dürrenmatt's grasp of his craft in the theoretical writings is not always reflected in the stage plays. We may be tempted to believe Dürrenmatt when he insists that he is a practitioner who develops his theories *post hoc* and derives them from the practical problems immediately facing him, but we must also take this assertion with a grain of salt. Since the publication of his essays it is clear that in many respects Dürrenmatt's understanding of problems preceded his mastery of the stage techniques necessary to present them successfully.

The successful presentation of tragedy and how it should be achieved have been constant concerns in most of Dürrenmatt's essays. In practice he has avoided the word tragedy and preferred to call his plays comedies, although they are clearly tragicomedies in which elements of both the tragic and comic reinforce each other. "But the tragic is still possible, even if pure tragedy is not. We can achieve the tragic out of comedy, produce it as a terrible moment, as an abyss that opens up. Indeed many tragedies of Shakespeare are comedies out of which the tragic arises." [30] The main device for causing the tragic to arise out of comedy is the "terrible moment," the "abyss that opens up," or in the word we have used, the grotesque, which Dürrenmatt here defines in passing.

Our world has led to the grotesque as well as to the atom bomb, and it is a world like that of Hieronymus Bosch, whose apocalyptic paintings are also grotesque. But the grotesque is only a visual expression, a visual paradox, the form of that which is formless, the face of a world without face, and just as thinking seems unable to get along without the concept of the paradox, so also art is dependent on paradox, and our world which still exists only because the atom bomb exists: out of fear of the bomb.[31]

The grotesque, the absolute paradox, is for Dürrenmatt never something that is merely ornamental; rather it is always the revelation of the "abyss" which is concealed by a veneer of civilization.

It is important to realize that there are two kinds of the grotesque: the grotesque for the sake of romanticism, one that wishes to awaken fear of strange emotions (for example, of having a ghost appear), and the grotesque for the sake of distance which can be achieved only by this means. . . . The grotesque is an extreme form of stylizing, an abrupt way of making things visual and therefore capable of coping with topical questions, or even with our present day without turning into slanted reportage. I could therefore imagine a shudderingly grotesque treatment of the second world war, but *not yet* a tragedy, since we do not yet have the requisite distance. . . . The grotesque is one of the great possibilities of being precise. It cannot be denied that this art possesses the cruelty of objectivity, yet it is not the art of nihilists, but rather that of moralists. . . .[32]

Dürrenmatt is a stern moralist, but one who does not wish to be caught in the act of moralizing. In a radio play like *Operation Vega* one may find the above quotations translated into dramatic action, for the play lives from the moral dilemma resulting from the paradoxical world situation of the atomic age. Less obvious and more indirect applications of the principles quoted may be found in most of his plays. The manner which we call typical of Dürrenmatt is to present the problems of our times in grotesque paradoxes. But in his theoretical writings the Swiss author prefers to avoid references to cosmic problems as themes for plays, nowhere refers to the "message" of a play, and is consistent in emphasizing that "the drama is bound to the presentation of human beings, and in every drama a world of human bodies is erected, for the building blocks of drama are people and always will be. To dramatize is synonymous with humanizing. . . ."[33] In the same essay he states that the "Theater is not pure literature, but poetry created by means of the art of acting. The art of drama is the depiction of human beings through the medium of the actor." The actor may interpret his role, but he does so by playing it, not by solving cosmic problems.

Taken as a whole, the theoretical writings constitute a series of revelations about Dürrenmatt's thinking about the world and about the theater. Inconsistencies may be found, and theses that are easy to refute; trivial statements alternate with profound comments that are significant for Dürrenmatt's growth as a dramatist. It is easy to disagree with many of his premises, but it is equally easy to accept most of his conclusions as reasonable statements. The validity of many of his assertions is, after all, not at stake, since the main interest lies with the discovery of Dürrenmatt's attitudes. His fame does not rest on his essays, interesting and provocative as many of these are. We must agree with Dürrenmatt that the proof of a play is in its stage success or failure. No number of "points" appended to a play as guidelines for its understanding will save it from failure with the public or rescue it from condemnation by the critics. Dürrenmatt is quite content that it should be so, for he, too, points to the primacy of practice and does not wish to be taken with deadly seriousness either in his plays or in his essays and lectures.[34] He remains a challenge to both critics and audiences, who must learn to laugh and understand at the same time. And as they learn, Dürrenmatt's fame and stature will increase.

Notes and References

Preface

1. The statistics are taken from *Cultural News from Germany* (Bonn, Inter Nationes). The three plays are: *The Visit*, 1958; *The Deadly Game* (by James Yaffe, based on Dürrenmatt's *Traps*), 1960; and *The Physicists*, 1965.

2. The six critics whose essays are included in *Der Unbequeme Dürrenmatt* approach the dramatist from different points of view but are in agreement that he is "uncomfortable," disquieting, and provocative.

Chapter One

1. *The City*, p. 15.
2. *Ibid.*, p. 25.
3. Wolfgang Kayser, *Das Groteske in Malerei und Dichtung* (The Grotesque in Art and Literature), Oldenburg, 1957; tr. U. Weisstein (Indiana University Press, 1963).
4. *Theater im Gespräch* (Theater Discussions), Munich, 1963, p. 277. She notes the uncomfortable feeling that results from even harmless grotesqueries and ascribes a feeling of relief and restoration to the laughter that ensues. This laughter, she asserts, is very different from that which is the response to intellectual sources and has little to do with what is termed comic or satirical. Reinhold Grimm, in his article "Parodie und Groteske im Werk Friedrich Dürrenmatts," considers the grotesque to be the basic formative element in all of Dürrenmatt's works and the attitude which stamps all the writings. But he wisely goes on to discuss the "playfully grotesque," pointing out that it plays as large a role as does the demonic kind. Grimm's observations are a good corrective to the notion, established by Kayser and upheld by Guthke, that the grotesque is primarily serious.
5. This is particularly true of Karl Guthke, whose careless use of terms invalidates, at times, his otherwise very important study of tragicomedy.
6. Wolfgang Hildescheimer, in *Akzente*, December, 1960. Cf. also Martin Esslin, *The Theater of the Absurd* (New York, 1961) and in

German the collection of essays *Sinn oder Unsinn?*, edited by Reinhold
Grimm *et al.* (Basel, 1962). The introduction by Klaus Völker is especially valuable for its definitions and delimitations of the grotesque in
drama. "The absurd theater does not show the world in its contradictions, it is only astonished at the contradictions and carries on its jokes.
The grotesque theater wishes to depict the madness that is going on"
(p. 11). Important also is Völker's statement that the term "grotesque"
does not specify a genre. In practice the tragicomedy is the genre
best adapted to the presentation of grotesque effects. "A grotesque
effect is felt by the spectator when a tragic event is presented on the
stage as comic. The comic and the tragic are intermingled like laughing and crying" (p. 10).

7. *The City*, p. 111.

8. Wellwarth, p. 14.

9. For further explication, Brock-Sulzer, p. 248, may be consulted.
She notes that direct expression is a constant temptation for Dürrenmatt. We might add that even in the later works he lapses into
expository prose.

10. Those interested in further discussion of this aspect of Dürrenmatt will find food for thought in Diller's essays, as well as in Buri's
essay in *Der Unbequeme Dürrenmatt.*

Chapter Two

1. For a retelling of the confused plot see Klarmann, pp. 105f.

2. The Dutchman Jan Bockelson (Johann von Leyden, 1509–36)
set up a theocracy in Münster in 1534–35. His regime showed some
primitive communist traits. Bockelson called himself "The King of the
New Zion." The Bishop of Münster, allied with the Landgrave of
Hessen, starved out the town after a long siege and captured it in
June, 1535. Bockelson was tortured with glowing tongs and his corpse
exhibited in a cage.

Biblical references: Matthew 19:30 and 20:16. Also Luke, 16 and
19—the Lazarus story.

3. The street-sweeper parodies *Faust*, I; the executioner, Schiller's
Wilhelm Tell and *The Bride of Messina.* For the importance of the
role of the executioner, see Allemann, pp. 427f. The two wives of the
Landgrave of Hessen repeat each other's words in a manner which
is mildly amusing, in the beginning, but soon becomes boring in its
mechanical clatter. Their speech is an early stage of the kind of comic
effect achieved by the choral speaking of the two castrati in *The Visit.*

4. Cf. Diller's article on Dürrenmatt's use of the stage. Diller suggests that the final tableau may be intended to convey "the plight of
men who, bound to earth, still futilely search the heavens for answers
to their greatest questions."

5. A crass example of this is found in *Comedies II*, p. 147. Part of this speech is translated by Klarmann, pp. 111f.

6. Also referred to are John 9:40 and Job 1:21.

7. *Writings on the Theater*, p. 106.

8. *Loc. cit.*, p. 113. Other critics concur. Miss Brock-Sulzer also sees the strong influence of the baroque drama, *loc. cit.*, p. 38.

9. *Writings on the Theater*, p. 205 (February, 1965).

Chapter Three

1. In spite of successful Swiss stagings, which established Dürrenmatt's reputation, the first production in Germany was a failure, and the play established itself slowly in that country. It is one of the most frequently performed of his plays and has been a favorite with college and university theaters in this country.

2. The subtitle is also ironic: "An Unhistorical Historical Comedy." There are several versions of this play: The first one, used for the *première* in Basel in 1949, has never been published. The second version, now published in *Comedies I*, is the version to which we refer. A third version has been published in *Spectaculum IV* (1961). Guthke refers to this play as a "comedy." But he overlooks the pathos of Romulus' personal sacrifice and the force of the conclusion. Properly understood, the work satisfies Guthke's own definition of the tragicomedy.

3. *Romulus* is one of the author's favorite plays, and in all the versions he has done nothing to soften the satire. The satiric thrusts at pompous nationalism and at a kind of militarism that is fond of heroic gestures have not endeared the play to some unreconstructed Germans.

4. Zeno did actually come from a region in Asia Minor called Isauria. The year 476 is correct, but the Ides of March are just a literary allusion. Romulus was actually a boy of about 14 years, whose father was called Orestes. Odoaker did give Romulus a pension and a fine villa near Naples. He was also killed by Theodoric, but they were not related. Domitian was the first emperor to pay tribute to Germanic tribes.

5. Wellwarth, p. 19.

6. Cf. *Writings on the Theater*, p. 206. Romulus' sincerity and conviction are, for Dürrenmatt, almost a sure guarantee of his failure.

7. *Comedies II*, p. 354. (Point nine of the notes appended to *The Physicists*.)

8. The figure of Oedipus stands behind such characters of Dürrenmatt's just as much as Don Quixote, if one accepts the interpretation that Oedipus used his best powers, his excellence (*arete*), to bring

about his own destruction, and that his excellence and ruin are two facets of the same thing.

9. Eric Bentley, in *The Playwright as Thinker*, p. 56, remarks: "In comedy we see and criticize man's life; in tragedy we sense and appraise his fate." Clearly we do both with regard to the figure of Romulus.

10. For an interesting analysis of the different versions of this play see Phelps's essay in *Modern Drama*, September, 1965, pp. 156f. A detailed special study is made by Heilmann in his essay "Tragic Elements in a Dürrenmatt Comedy," *Modern Drama*, May, 1967, pp. 11f.

11. In his article, Wellwarth (p. 20) suggests: "Dürrenmatt has created as banal a plot as possible in order to fix the audience's attention while he exposes the characters and philosophies of his protagonists."

12. *Comedies I*, pp. 95–96.

13. The critics are unanimous in seeing her as modeled on Frank Wedekind's Lulu, from the play of that name. In our play she represents the incalculable force of chance that brings to nought the best-laid plans. In his book Jauslin gives the essentials of the attempts by Wedekind's widow to sue Dürrenmatt for plagiarism. Dürrenmatt answered the charge in an essay "Confessions of a Plagiarist," first published in *Die Tat* (Zurich), August 9, 1952, and now available in *Writings on the Theater*, pp. 239f. Dürrenmatt's essay also contains interesting comments on his intentions in writing *Mississippi*, although proving again that an author is not always his own best interpreter.

14. The stage directions which precede the play are fun to read but impossible to realize in a literal sense. What should a director do with the remark: "The room stinks to high heaven"? For Dürrenmatt's own view of the problems of staging, see *Writings on the Theater*, pp. 104f.

15. *Comedies I*, p. 86.

16. Urs Jenny (p. 41) points out that even in the stage directions surcharged, extravagant language is used.

17. Cf. Brock-Sulzer, pp. 66f.

18. The play was originally intended to be part of a sequence of plays on the theme of the Tower of Babel. Our references are to the second version of 1957, now in *Comedies I*. One may refer to the author's note appended to the play, p. 263. For a discussion of the different versions see Jauslin, pp. 74f.

19. For Dürrenmatt's own view of the setting and the primacy of place in the drama, see *Writings on the Theater*, pp. 104f.

20. "Was bleibt stifte ich den Dichtern," Akki remarks, neatly inverting Hölderlin's famous lines from the poem "Andenken": "Was bleibet aber, stiften die Dichter."

21. For some critics, all of Dürrenmatt's plays are religious parables that must be analyzed for their message and tested for their doctrinal content. For others his plays are merely blasphemous. The *Aachener Volkszeitung* of November 20, 1964 writes about a television broadcast of our play: "Dürrenmatt's comedy is an anti-religious play that mixes, with refined artistic skill, sociological criticism and sarcastic blasphemy."

22. *Comedies I*, p. 177. "What has been created is good, and what is good is happy."

23. The subtitle, "A Tragic Comedy," is always mentioned in studies of the play, which has stimulated much research in the genre of tragicomedy. Guthke (p. 36) offers a definition of tragicomedy which may be briefly summarized as follows: the elements of tragedy and comedy are so fused that each serves to intensify and support the other. Guthke, however, goes on to postulate a "grotesque" play, a genre which in fact does not exist, since "grotesque" is not a structural category. Guthke tends to confuse "grotesque" and "absurd." For a correction of his view, consult Jauslin, p. 124.

24. Ian Loram's essay is a fine study of the relation of Valency's *The Visit* to the original text. But Loram has been too kind to Valency, whose distortions of the original are inexcusable. Perhaps the most damaging change made in the adaptation was the refashioning of the end of the second act. The English version shows quite unmotivated changes in Schill (Ill), which Dürrenmatt saves for the third act.

25. The name Güllen is derived from "Gülle," meaning either urine or puddle. As in all his plays, Dürrenmatt has chosen amusing or suggestive names for his characters. Ill has no significance in German. Clara Wäscher is supposed to suggest a member of the lower class; Claire's married name, Zachanassian, may echo Onassis. Ill's first name, Alfred, is neutral in itself, but is also the first name of the hero of *Traps*, a work composed at the same time.

26. This is a very important difference from the English adaptation.

27. *Comedies I*, pp. 357–59. Cf. *ibid.*, p. 357: "I am describing people, not puppets, an action, not an allegory, and am establishing a world not a moral. . . ."; "Play what is obvious correctly and the depth dimensions will emerge by themselves."; "Claire Zachanassian represents neither justice nor the Marshall Plan nor the apocalypse; let her be just that which she is, namely the richest woman in the world who is enabled by her money to act like the heroine of a Greek tragedy, absolutely, cruelly, perhaps like Medea."; "It is a community which slowly yields to temptation, like the teacher, yet this yielding must be understandable. The temptation is too great, the poverty is too bitter. The Old Lady is a malicious play, but just for that reason it must be presented without anger and in the most humane way, with

sadness yet with humor, for nothing hurts this comedy that ends tragically more than brutal seriousness."

28. The basis of the play as re-enactment of ritual has been so carefully and convincingly worked out by Melvin W. Askew that to avoid repeating his presentation we refer the student to his article in *The Tulane Drama Review*. I have borrowed some of his main points. It must be understood, however, that Dürrenmatt's primary purpose is to present a dramatic course of action. Therefore parallels in myth and legend must merely be taken as possible analogies.

29. For a review of the consensus on this point consult Miss Hortenbach's essay in *Monatshefte*. Some critics, such as Diller, insist throughout on theological interpretations of all that Dürrenmatt has written. Diller is both the most consistent and the most insistent in this regard. A discussion of a Dürrenmatt play which starts with the theological significance and the metaphysical framework may easily turn into philosophizing on the meaning or message of the play to the detriment, if not the total neglect, of its dramatic structure and stage presence. Holzapfel, for example, speaks of Claire as "the agent who cleanses Ill of his sins," a fine example of systematic error and the compulsion of a conceptual schematism. Theological discussions of the plays tend not only to be humorless, which is inappropriate for comedies, but are also prone to grandiose conceptual schemes with only tenuous ties to the plays themselves. Let us not forget that Dürrenmatt uses the word "comedy" in most of his titles. Let us also take Dürrenmatt seriously, if not too naïvely so, when he stresses the stageworthiness of his plays rather than their "moral." Most of the plays are hilarious comedies; an audience that fails to laugh has not grasped the play. Criticism of Dürrenmatt should not bring to his plays more deadly seriousness than Dürrenmatt himself demonstrates in them. It may be that to consign to footnotes all theological considerations is most apposite and in the spirit of the author. At the other extreme, it is also possible to miss any serious content if one is disturbed by the jokes. A sad example of this tendency may be observed in Heinz Beckmann, *Nach dem Spiel*, p. 150.

30. Hortenbach, *loc. cit.*, p. 147. Later in the same essay the author states: "Claire's role as God is the precondition for the drama proper." Considerable evidence is adduced to buttress this dry assertion, which is patent nonsense. Claire's power and justice are parodies of divine power and justice as well as perversions of their human counterpart. In the spirit of the critics mentioned above, one could argue that Claire is an agent of the divine order in spite of her repellent qualities. But this soon leads to philosophical abstractions. One should not lose one's sense of humor in the perusal of a Dürrenmatt play.

31. *Writings on the Theater,* pp. 186–88.

32. Except, of course, for Miss Brock-Sulzer, who always emphasizes the positive aspects of Dürrenmatt's works.

33. Our references are to the version printed in *Comedies II.*

34. In *The Visit* the world was reduced to business by Claire. In *Frank V* the business sphere is taken as a model for the world.

35. Cf. *Writings on the Theater,* p. 190. Frank the Fifth is a spineless lover of the classics who uses literature as an escape from reality and as an idle embellishment of leisure hours.

36. *Ibid.,* p. 190f. The text also refers to "heroes from Shakespeare."

37. *Comedies II,* p. 252.

38. In his interview with Horst Bienek, Dürrenmatt said of his play: "*Frank V* is an experiment in pure drama. . . . The songs do not give the play a thrust in the direction of generality, as in *The Three Penny Opera,* but in the direction of the tolerable. . . . In *Frank* the people sing when they are lying . . . I am not representing a capitalistic society but rather a coercive system. In general Freedom is the real problem of the play, and not justice as in *The Old Lady.*"

39. In several interviews Dürrenmatt has said that the role of the psychiatrist was originally written for a man, but that it was rewritten for a woman when an actress friend asked him to let her play the part. The play is now published with the dedication "for Therese Giese."

40. *Comedies II,* p. 343.

41. This thesis is more eloquently stated in Dürrenmatt's *Problems of the Theater.* Obviously the effect of this belief, if carried to its extreme, is that only private solutions can be achieved in modern drama.

42. Now published in *Writings on the Theater,* pp. 272f.

43. *Ibid.,* p. 275.

44. *Ibid.,* p. 276: "That everything is understandable in human terms makes the story so devilish."

45. Some of the more important "points": 1. I do not proceed from a thesis, but from a story. 3. A story has been thought through to the end when it has taken the worst possible turn. 4. The worst possible turn is not predictable. It comes about by chance. 5. The art of the dramatist consists in applying chance in an action in the most effective way. 6. The agents of the dramatic action are people. 8. The more according to plan people proceed, the more effectively chance can strike them. 9. People who proceed according to plan wish to attain a definite goal. Chance strikes them worst when because of chance they achieve the opposite of their goal: that which they feared and sought to avoid (for example, Oedipus). 10. Such a story is, to be sure, grotesque, but not absurd (contrary to sense).

46. Since the more significant version of the story is represented

by the radio play, our comments here are concerned chiefly with the reasons for the failure of the stage version. A detailed comparison of the two versions may be found in Brock-Sulzer, pp. 142–43.

47. Or the third labor, depending on which version of the myth one follows. Dürrenmatt presumably relies on Gustav Schwab's famous retelling. The labor of the Augean stables is often the sixth in sequence. But this is obviously a minor point.

48. Dürrenmatt makes free use of the legend to enhance his satire. There are also some sly allusions, as, for example, to Hercules' virility; he is said to have had eighty sons.

49. *Comedies II*, p. 397. What originally had been a satiric battle with the bureaus has been turned into a reminiscence of Socrates' message in the *Crito*.

50. The message of readiness for grace, if it should come, is reminiscent of several of Rilke's *New Poems*. If this is indeed an echo of Rilke, it is the only one I have noted.

51. *Comedies II*, p. 410. The didactic tone of this sermon is all the more surprising in view of the comic possibilities that might have been exploited.

52. Heinz Beckmann, who can be counted on to misunderstand every Dürrenmatt play, outdoes himself in a review in *Rheinischer Merkur*, January 28, 1966: "Jokes, jokes, and cynical wit, and all for the moment." Elements of wit seem to throw the humorless Beckmann into disarray, causing him to lose the thread of the action and the sense of a play after the first joke.

53. *The New York Times*, October 18, 1964; interview with Jean-Pierre Lenoir in Rottach, Germany.

54. *Der Meteor*, p. 67.

55. This is the sense of the scene with Nyffenschwander, which reaches its high point on p. 46.

56. *Ibid.*, p. 68.

57. *Ibid.*, p. 69.

58. *Ibid.*, p. 48. On p. 65 there is a possible echo of *Frank V:* "One needs education in order to make bigger deals with less risk than would ever be possible by criminal action."

59. *Writings on the Theater*, p. 283.

60. Cf. point 8. At present the only source for these "points" is the *Neue Zürcher Zeitung*, February 28, 1966. For that reason they are appended here. 1. Criticism without analysis is impossible. 2. It is a question of what the author represents on the stage and not of what the author intended. What the author intended is his affair; what he presents is the objective result of his efforts. Criticism should concern itself first of all with this result. 3. The objective result is to be examined for its immanent logic. For example, nothing may happen in a

play without reason. The reason why something happens must lie in the idea of the play. But not only the basis of the action, but also the personalities depicted must be determined by the idea of the play. 4. The idea of a play must or should by itself contain the dramatic configuration which makes the play possible. A play has no other statement than its idea—or expressed differently, all its statements must have their basis in the idea. 5. The idea of the play is the story of a man who is resurrected and who does not believe his resurrection. 6. A resurrection is a miracle. 7. A miracle is twofold: for the believer it is a proof of God; for the non-believer, it is an unknown phenomenon of nature, a hallucination, a deception, that is, a scandal. 8. The resurrected man who does not believe in his resurrection is therefore a double scandal: for some he is a scandal *qua* resurrected person, and for others, as a person who does not believe. 9. The reason why *The Meteor* is a scandal, therefore, lies in the idea of the play: the scandal is unavoidable. 10. A resurrected person who does not believe in his resurrection is a paradox. 11. A paradoxical person is, in a higher sense, a comic figure, a figure which is at one and the same time tragic and comic. *The Meteor* is conceivable neither as pure comedy nor as pure tragedy. Above all, the idea, if one dares to present it, will stand no toning down in the direction of moralistic Christianity. Being tragic and comic at the same time does not mean that the tragic and comic elements cancel each other out, but rather that they confront each other quite abruptly—which is also a problem for the staging. *The Meteor* cannot stand a polished staging—it is a wild play. 12. As a resurrected person who does not believe in his resurrection, Schwitter is a figure of the Christian Western world. Through the occurrence of a miracle a fact is posited. Christianity believes in the promised resurrection of man at the Last Judgment—the question is only to what degree Christians today believe it. Originally, Christendom was conscious of being a stumbling block for Jews and a folly for Greeks. Today it is upset by the fact that it is supposed to be a folly for non-Christians: modern Christianity has become a stumbling block for itself. Seen from this perspective, the resurrected person who does not believe in his resurrection is a figure who symbolizes modern Christianity. Inasmuch as we are members of modern Christianity, we are laughing, scoffing, and becoming annoyed with ourselves. 13. When I call Schwitter a figure of the Christian Western world, I don't mean that he is an allegory and I also do not mean that I have written an allegorical tale, in which everything has some deeper meaning—like that lady who said, after Eliot's *Cocktail Party*, that she had understood everything, except when the psychiatrist said to Celia "Sit down" she had missed the deeper meaning. *Hamlet* or *Lear* are no allegories either, and yet their characters are valid images of a basic human situation. 14. The resurrected person who does not believe in his resurrection cannot believe. *The Meteor* is a play about the inability to believe. A resurrected person cannot know one thing: the fact that he was dead. The fact that he was dead he must find out from other people. Therefore he must believe others. To believe means, in its primary, primitive sense, to trust others. By not trusting others, one isolates oneself. Not-believing is isolation. Schwitter is isolated; he is a separate person; and in his horrible loneliness he is an image of the separate person. 15. The resurrected person who does not believe in his resurrection is a paradox. He does not know that he believes in something wrong. He considers his belief to be knowledge. For him death is something insuperable. He does not believe in his resurrection because he does not believe in resurrection in general. He has nothing but life. His despair is the fact that he must die. If he wants to overcome his despair, he must invest death with some meaning. He can only do that—from an extreme point of view, and *The Meteor* is only meaningful as an extreme play—by questioning life and positing death as the Absolute. Only in this way does dying become the climax of life. 16. Man does not live alone. Life is only possible through and in life—man is alone only when dying. Dying is the last possible isolation. In dying, man becomes a total individual. Schwitter isolates himself twice: by not believing and by believing that he is dying. 17. As a resurrected person, Schwitter belongs to the living—as a resurrected person who does not believe in his resurrection, he is numbered among the dying. He becomes an isolated individual in society and a total individual among those who are only relatively individual: such an individual becomes dangerous because the death in which he believes does not take place. 18. Schwitter does not attain eternal life but rather eternal dying. 19. That is the idea of the play in its discussable form. Only on this basis can the play be criticized, that is to say, scrutinized. 20. A play is the transformation of an idea into something absolutely spontaneous.

61. Utnapuschtim in *An Angel* is merely funny in his mouthings of propaganda and in his trimming. The pastor in *The Visit* is more sharply satirized and more severely condemned for being ineffectual. The missionary in *The Physicists* is weak and ludicrous, and remains a figure of comic relief. Not until *The Meteor* did Dürrenmatt show a clergyman who was capable of doubts and suffering and thereby acquired sympathetic traits which raise him above a mere caricature.

62. Most vehemently and with the least understanding, Urs Jenny in *Theater Heute,* April, 1967, pp. 11f. As early as 1959, Dürrenmatt had speculated on the role of miracles in modern dramaturgy. "Thus a miracle must be consciously *not* motivated, as something inherently incomprehensible, or the meaning of the miracle must be very clearly

worked out, especially of course, if it happens twice." (*Writings on the Theater*, p. 283.) And in the same context: "Basically a miracle means a test or an opportunity, but always an aid to belief or the confirmation of belief."

63. Schumacher, with a punning reference to a short story of Dürrenmatt's, entitles his essay "The Poet as His Own Executioner." Although one must discount much of his adverse criticism because of the crassly Communist approach, Schumacher is right in considering the play as an ultimate negation of literature that permits no further development.

Chapter Four

1. Most American textbooks discuss the definition and the esthetic principles of the play in their introductions. Perhaps the best introduction is that by Frederick G. Goldberg in *Spiegel und Echo: Fünf deutsche Hörspiele.* (New York: Harcourt, Brace and World, 1965).

2. *Writings on the Theater*, p. 55.

3. The June, 1959, issue of the periodical *Akzente* offered a panel discussion of the place of the parable in recent literature. Among the authors cited are Kafka, Brecht, and James Joyce. A general tendency to return to the form of the parable is noted as a characteristic of the literature of the 1950's. In general one may say that most modern writers assume the truth and acceptability of the moral contained in the parable. It is this which distinguishes modern parables from nineteenth-century thesis plays. If one adds an ironic inversion of normal values, then a useful formula for Dürrenmatt's non-didactic radio plays has been found. Parabolic scenes are a means of demonstrating a moral or thesis rather than acting out a dramatic process, so that the language tends to become a discussion rather than a dramatic dialogue.

4. Louis MacNeice, "Varieties of Parable," in *The Clark Lectures, 1963*, Cambridge [England] University Press, 1965, p. 9. He goes on to note that fairy tales can be well dramatized for the radio. Cf. also *Essays on Contemporary German Literature*, IV, 13.

5. *Writings on the Theater*, p. 61.

6. The most pertinent passages are: "Therefore as sin came into the world through one man and death through sin. . . ." "Abraham believed God, and it was reckoned to him as righteousness." "Then as one man's trespass led to condemnation for all men, so one man's act of righteousness leads to acquittal and life for all men."

7. According to Bänziger, p. 166, it was written during the 1940's. The work properly belongs to Dürrenmatt's practice prose. In 1960 it was published in book form. It now forms the first play in the volume *Radio Plays*.

8. Cf. p. 137, where the announcer reports, with gentle irony, that "a miracle had happened . . ."

9. Eugen Kurt Fischer, *Das Hörspiel*, Stuttgart: Kröner, 1964.

10. *Radio Plays*, p. 199.

11. For the American student of German the derivatives have some linguistic interest. Some of the compounds are: *ausmisten, vermisten, entmisten, Oberausmister*.

12. Heinrich Böll's *Ein Schluck Erde* (*A Taste of Earth*) is another typical negative utopia with a similar message. The following quotation is taken from *Radio Plays*, p. 221.

13. *Die Heimat im Plakat* (Zurich, 1963) is a book of drawings in which Dürrenmatt vents his spleen on the subject in a playful—but serious—manner.

14. The well-known author and translator Richard Winston has suggested to me that this introductory section, with its crabbed syntax and erratic sequence of thoughts, may be a parody of Faulkner. Whatever the target, the reader feels the parodistic thrust as well as the self-directed irony.

Chapter Five

1. Gillis' essay, "Dürrenmatt and the Detectives" is a brief but competent study of the stories of this genre.

2. To give just one example instead of many: the bishop speaks of the bride as one "whom all present have taken to their hearts" and who "has given so much love." As an example of the use of leitmotifs, we may note that Archilochos seems to be pursued by pictures and statues of naked men and women. Even when on his way to attack the president he climbs up statues of naked women. The leitmotif has two functions, the first and obvious one being the contrast with Archilochos' innocence and inexperience in love. But nakedness is, of course, also appropriate to a Greek story and is part of the stylistic spoof on Dürrenmatt's part.

Chapter Six

1. Not only drama critics and reviewers have found it a mine of information and a source of valuable opinions. Wolfgang Kayser, in his book on the grotesque, refers to and quotes from it. Some passages have become famous through frequent quotations. Our references are to the volume of critical writings edited by Brock-Sulzer, pp. 92–132.

2. All references are to this volume.

3. That this is a deliberate policy is evident from *Writings on the Theater*, pp. 171f.

4. *Writings on the Theater*, p. 174.

5. *Ibid.*, p. 148.

6. *Ibid.* p. 156; cf. Urs Jenny, p. 94.

7. Züfle notes that "gray theory has become increasingly the accompaniment to his stage plays," *loc. cit.,* p. 38. The specific reference is to *The Meteor,* but the remark is valid for the period since the Statement of Position appended to *Frank V.* The failure of this play marks a turning point in Dürrenmatt's career. Since 1960 he has felt it necessary to be his own interpreter to a much greater degree than previously.

8. Cf. i.a., *Writings on the Theater,* p. 170. In an interview published in the *Aachener Volkszeitung* in January, 1965, he stated: "I am much less satiric than humorous. The critics are often unjust in this connection and fail to understand me. But criticism is after all unjust by nature—I too have been unfair in criticizing."

9. Walter Kerr's book, *Tragedy and Comedy* (New York: Simon and Schuster, 1967), develops this thesis eloquently and at length.

10. Classic in this respect is the long interview with Horst Bienek in *Workshop Conversations.*

11. *Writings on the Theater,* pp. 162f.

12. *Ibid.,* p. 168.

13. *Ibid.,* p. 87: "The stage scenery can falsify a play." This was written in 1947–48.

14. *Ibid.,* p. 118.

15. *Ibid.,* pp. 119f.

16. *Ibid.,* p. 122.

17. He is also quick to qualify and tone down statements which might seem in isolation to be too drastic. Thus he goes on (p. 122) to state that comedy and tragedy are really only points of view.

18. *Ibid.,* p. 92. The "Statement of Position," p. 187, is also pertinent here.

19. *Ibid.,* p. 62.

20. "Precision and style of language are determined by the degree of logic immanent in its content. One cannot work on language, but only on thought, and one works on thought by means of language." *Ibid.,* p. 62.

21. His insistence on "invented" plot is buttressed by his references to Aristophanes, who did not dramatize well-known legends, but invented plots, that is, proceeded from "Einfall" to "Einfall." Cf. *ibid.,* pp. 132f.

22. *Ibid.,* p. 56.

23. *Ibid.,* p. 60.

24. In the interview referred to in note 8 above, he makes a distinction between "religious" and "theological." "I am religious. If one has a sense of humor, one must be religious. But I am not theological."

25. *Writings on the Theater,* p. 128.

26. *Ibid.*, pp. 44 and 130. It would be unfair to a writer as witty as Dürrenmatt not to add that he is capable of less highflown remarks on the rationale of creative writing: "Earning money is a prime stimulus for writers" (*ibid.*, p. 55).

27. Bienek, *op. cit.*, p. 106. *Writings on the Theater*, p. 72: "Only the comedian's comedy may still be adequate to the situation." And p. 73: ". . . for the theater is by nature comical," since it is not the world nor even an image of it, but a free and freely imagined world. And in the same context: "The moral of the theater lies not in its attempted but in its unintentional morality."

28. Just before the passage quoted Dürrenmatt states his belief in a "naïve" public that seeks help and advice.

29. *Ibid.*, pp. 48–49.

30. *Ibid.*, pp. 122–23.

31. *Ibid.*, p. 122.

32. *Ibid.*, pp. 136–37.

33. *Ibid.*, p. 161.

34. *Ibid.*, pp. 71–72.

Selected Bibliography

1. Works

Komödien I (*Comedies I*). Zurich: Arche, 1967. Second edition 1958. Contains: *Romulus the Great, The Marriage of Mr. Mississippi, An Angel Comes to Babylon,* and *The Visit.*

Komödien II (*Comedies II*). Zurich: Arche, 1963. Contains: *It Is Written, The Blind Man, Frank V, The Physicists,* and *Hercules and the Augean Stables.*

Der Meteor (*The Meteor*). Zurich: Arche, 1966.

Hörspiele (*Radio Plays*). Zurich: Arche, 1963. Contains: *The Double, The Case of the Donkey's Shadow, Nocturnal Talk with a Despised Person, Stranitzky and the National Hero, Hercules and the Augean Stables, Operation Vega, Traps,* and *An Evening in Late Fall.*

Theaterschriften und Reden (*Writings on the Theater*), ed. Elisabeth Brock-Sulzer. Zurich: Arche, 1966.

Die Stadt (*The City*). Zurich: Arche, 1962.

"Der Richter und sein Henker" ("The Judge and His Executioner"). 2nd ed. Zurich: Arche, 1957.

"Der Verdacht" ("The Suspicion"). Zurich: Benziger, 1953.

"Die Panne" ("Traps"). Zurich: Arche, 1956.

"Das Versprechen" ("The Pledge"). Zurich: Arche, 1958.

"Griechе sucht Griechin" ("Once a Greek"). Frankfurt: Ullstein, 1961.

Die Heimat im Plakat (*Our Country in Placards*). Zurich: Diogenes, 1963.

2. School Texts

Der Besuch der alten Dame, ed. Paul Kurt Ackermann. Boston: Houghton Mifflin Co. n.d.

Romulus der Grosse, ed. H. F. Garten. Boston: Houghton Mifflin Co., 1962.

Die Physiker, ed. Robert Helbling. New York: Oxford University Press, 1965.

Drei Hörspiele, ed. Henry Regensteiner. New York: Holt, Rinehart

and Winston, 1965. (*Evening in Late Fall, The Double, Traps.*)
Der Richter und sein Henker, ed. William Gillis and John Neumaier.
Boston: Houghton Mifflin Co., 1961.
Der Verdacht, ed. William Gillis. Boston: Houghton Mifflin Co., 1964.
Die Panne in: *Spiegel der Zeit,* ed. Paulene H. Roth and M. L. Nielsen. Houghton Mifflin Co., 1960.

3. Bibliographies

Wilbert-Collins, Elly. *A Bibliography of Four Contemporary German-Swiss Authors.* Amsterdam: Erasmus, 1967.
PETTERSEN, K. D. *Dürrenmatt-Bibliographie.* Bad Homburg, 1967.
(vol. III of Bibliographien zum Studium der deutschen Sprache und Literatur.)

4. Translations

FRIEDRICH DÜRRENMATT. *Four Plays 1957–62.* London, 1964. Contains: *Problems of the Theater,* tr. Gerhard Nellhaus; *Romulus the Great, The Marriage of Mr. Mississippi, An Angel Comes to Babylon,* and *The Physicists.*
The Physicists, tr. James Kirkup. New York: Grove Press, 1964.
The Visit, tr. Patrick Bowles. London, 1962.
"The Judge and His Hangman," tr. Therese Pol. New York: Dolphin Books, 1963.
"The Pledge," tr. Richard and Clara Winston. New York: Knopf, 1959. Signet Books, 1960.
"Traps," tr. Richard and Clara Winston. New York: Knopf, 1960.
"Once a Greek," tr. Richard and Clara Winston. New York: Knopf, 1965.
An Angel Comes to Babylon: Romulus the Great. New York: Grove Press, 1966.
"The Marriage of Mr. Mississippi." A Play, and "Problems of the Theater." An Essay, tr. Michael Bullock. New York: Grove Press, 1966.
Incident at Twilight in: *Postwar German Theatre,* ed. and tr. Michael Benedict and George E. Wellwarth. New York: E. P. Dutton, 1967.

5. Critical Studies

BÄNZIGER, HANS. *Frisch und Dürrenmatt.* 4th ed. Berne: France, 1965.
This has become the best-known reference work.
BECKMANN, HEINZ. *Nach dem Spiel.* Munich: Albert Langen, 1963.
BIENEK, HORST. *Werkstattgespräche mit Schriftstellern.* Munich, 1962.
BROCK-SULZER, ELISABETH. *Friedrich Dürrenmatt: Stationen seines*

Werkes. Zurich: Arche, 1964. Invariably laudatory, but with many good insights.

DIETRICH, MARGRET. *Das moderne Drama.* Stuttgart: Kröner, 1961. Deals with movements in European drama; an interesting comparative study of modern drama and dramatic theory.

FISCHER, E. K. *Das Hörspiel.* Stuttgart: Kröner, 1964. The best short introduction to the theory and practice of radio plays.

GRIMM, REINHOLD, ed. *Der unbequeme Dürrenmatt.* Stuttgart: Basilius-Presse, 1962. Important collection of essays by various critics.

————. *Sinn oder Unsinn? Das Groteske in modernen Drama.* Stuttgart: Basilius-Presse, 1962. Dürrenmatt is discussed, among other German authors, in an essay by Klaus Völker.

GUTHKE, KARL S. *Geschichte und Poetik der deutschen Tragikomödie.* Göttingen: Vandenhoeck & Ruprecht, 1961. The most complete and thorough study of its kind. Important for its definitions and analyses.

————. *Modern Tragicomedy: An Investigation into the Nature of the Genre.* New York: Random House, 1966. Theoretical portions are similar to those of the German book, but the scope of authors chosen is much wider.

HAMMER, CARL, ed. *Studies in German Literature.* Baton Rouge: Louisiana State University Press, 1963. Interesting essay on modern German drama by F. E. Coenen.

JAUSLIN, CHRISTIAN. *Friedrich Dürrenmatt: Zur Struktur seiner Dramen.* Zurich: Juris, 1964. Detailed, thorough analysis; the best of its kind.

JENNY, URS. *Friedrich Dürrenmatt.* Velber: Friedrich, 1965. Popularizing and journalistic.

KESTING, MARIANNE. *Panorama des zeitgenössischen Theaters.* Munich: Piper, 1962. Short, factual section on Dürrenmatt.

MAYER, HANS. *Dürrenmatt und Frisch.* Pfullingen: Neske, 1965.

SHAW, LEROY, ed. *The German Theater Today.* Austin: University of Texas Press, 1963. Interesting symposium and valuable introduction to the subject for American students.

STRELKA, JOSEPH. *Brecht, Horvath, Dürrenmatt.* Vienna, 1962.

SYBERBERG, HANS-JÜRGEN. *Zum Drama Friedrich Dürrenmatts.* Munich: UNI-Druck, 1963. Detailed analysis of *The Visit* and *Romulus.*

6. Articles in English

ASKEW, MELVIN W. "Dürrenmatt's *The Visit of the Old Lady,*" *Tulane Drama Review,* No. 4 (June, 1961), pp. 89–105. Best study of the play as re-enactment of ritual.

DAVIAU, DONALD G., "Justice in the Works of Friedrich Dürrenmatt,"

Kentucky Foreign Language Quarterly, IX (1962), 181–93.
Based mostly on the early works and radio plays.

DILLER, EDWARD, "Human Dignity in a Materialistic Society: Friedrich Dürrenmatt and Bertholt Brecht," *Modern Language Quarterly* XXV (1964), 451–60.

———. "Dürrenmatt's Use of the Stage as a Dramatic Element," *Symposium*, XX (1966), 197–206.

———. "Aesthetics and the Grotesque: Friedrich Dürrenmatt," *Wisconsin Studies in Contemporary Literature*, VII (1966), pp. 328–335.

———. "Despair and the Paradox: Friedrich Dürrenmatt," *Drama Survey*, V (1966), 131–36.

———. "Friedrich Dürrenmatt's Theological Concept of History," *German Quarterly*, XL (1967), 363–71.

GILLIS, WILLIAM. "Dürrenmatt and the Detectives," *German Quarterly* (1962), 71–74. Still the best study of the subject.

HEILMANN, ROBERT B. "The Lure of the Demonic: James and Dürrenmatt," *Comparative Literature*, XIII (1961), 346–57.

———. "Dürrenmatt's Tragic Comedy," *Modern Drama*, X (1967), 11–16. Interesting examination of *Mississippi*.

HOLZAPFEL, ROBERT. "The Divine Plan Behind the Plays of Friedrich Dürrenmatt," *Modern Drama*, VIII (1965), 237–46.

HORTENBACH, JENNY C. "Biblical Echoes in Dürrenmatt's *Der Besuch der alten Dame*," *Monatshefte* (1965), 145–61.

JOHNSON, PETER. "Grotesqueness and Injustice in Dürrenmatt," *German Life and Letters*, XV (1961), 264–73.

KIRCHBERGER, LIDA. "'Kleider machen Leute' and Dürrenmatt's *Panne*," *Monatshefte*, LII (1960), 1–8.

KLARMANN, ADOLF D. "Friedrich Dürrenmatt and the Tragic Sense of Comedy," *Modern Drama: Essays in Criticism*, ed. Travis Bogard and William Oliver. New York: Oxford University Press, 1965.

LORAM, IAN C. "*Der Besuch der alten Dame* and *The Visit*," *Monatshefte*, LIII (1961), 15–21.

PEPPARD, MURRAY B. "The Grotesque in Dürrenmatt's Dramas," *Kentucky Foreign Language Quarterly*, IX (1962), 36–44.

PHELPS, LELAND R., "Dürrenmatt's *Die Ehe des Herrn Mississippi*: The Revision of a Play," *Modern Drama*, VIII (1965), 156–60.

REED, EUGENE E., "The Image of the Unimaginable: A Note on Dürrenmatt's *Der Richter und sein Henker*," *Revue des Langues Vivantes*, No. 2 (1961), pp. 117–23.

———. "Dürrenmatt's *Der Besuch der alten Dame*: A Study in the Grotesque," *Monatshefte*, LIII (1961), 9–14.

SCHWARZ, ALFRED, "Toward a Poetic of Modern Realistic Tragedy," *Modern Drama* (1966), 136–46.

SHEPPARD, VERA, "Friedrich Dürrenmatt as a Dramatic Theorist," *Drama Survey*, IV (1965), 244–63.
THOMPSON, WILLIAM I. "Freedom and Comedy," *Tulane Drama Review*, IX (1965), 216–28.
VALENCY, MAURICE. *"The Visit*—A Modern Tragedy," *Theatre Arts*, May, 1958, pp. 17, 90–91.
WAIDSON, H. M. "Friedrich Dürrenmatt," in *German Men of Letters*, vol. III, ed. Alex Nathan. Philadelphia, 1964.
WELLWARTH, GEORGE. "Friedrich Dürrenmatt and Max Frisch: Two Views of the Drama," *Tulane Drama Review* (March, 1962), pp. 14–42.

Index

155

74385

DATE DUE

GAYLORD			PRINTED IN U.S.A.